Living God's Future Now

Living God's Future Now

Conversations with Contemporary Prophets

Edited by

Samuel Wells

CANTERBURY
PRESS
Norwich

© the Editor and Contributors 2022

First published in 2022 by the Canterbury Press Norwich
Editorial office
3rd Floor, Invicta House
108–114 Golden Lane
London EC1Y 0TG, UK
www.canterburypress.co.uk

Canterbury Press is an imprint of Hymns Ancient & Modern Ltd
(a registered charity)

Hymns Ancient & Modern® is a registered trademark of
Hymns Ancient & Modern Ltd
13A Hellesdon Park Road, Norwich,
Norfolk NR6 5DR, UK

British Library Cataloguing in Publication data

A catalogue record for this book is available
from the British Library

978 1-78622-415-6

Typeset by Regent Typesetting
Printed and bound in Great Britain by
CPI Group (UK) Ltd

Contents

Preface

When the pandemic took hold in the UK in March 2020, HeartEdge was transformed from a face-to-face renewal movement into a permanent online festival of ideas, seminars, workshops and debate. Its emphasis on the four Cs – commerce, compassion, culture and congregational life – remained, but within a fortnight it began to be conducted through online platforms and with a larger, international participant and contributor circle.

It quickly became clear that what was needed was a focal moment that crystallized what HeartEdge had almost overnight become – not just a forum for fostering, enhancing and dispersing ideas about mission and ministry, but a theatre for rehearsing insights about the great issues on everybody's minds – the pandemic, most obviously, and the climate crisis, which seemed so different from the perspective of lockdown, but also after the murder of George Floyd a heightened awareness of racialized justice, and before and after the US presidential election the fragility of democracy.

Thus from May 2020 to October 2021, each second Thursday evening, I entered conversation with a sequence of contemporary prophets, seeking their wisdom and perspective on these and other issues raised by their context and mine, and those of the participants, who had the opportunity to ask questions of their own. None of us knew the shape of the pandemic or how long the series would continue; those we invited were figures who we felt we'd be glad to join in conversation in any context, but who we felt had particular things to say in this one. Their experiences reflect the breadth of the themes of HeartEdge – commerce, compassion, culture and congregational life – and also the issues most discussed among our various HeartEdge forums during the period.

Each event was a conversation rather than an interview. I contributed my own reflections as well as drawing thoughts from my conversation partner. When we had the idea of turning these conversations into a book – after the first year or so – it became clear the nature of a chapter is different from simply a transcribed conversation. Thus I have edited out my own voice from the chapters, while reflecting my thoughts in some of the directions my companions' thoughts take. This is less about modesty than about making a more satisfying experience for the reader. To add a little of my own voice, I've included an Introduction, which began as a sermon given in an empty church during the second lockdown, and an Epilogue, which is an address I gave on Zoom to the ChurchWorks Commission for Covid Recovery during the omicron outbreak.

Chapter 5, in addition to being longer, has a different shape from the others. The conversation with Stanley Hauerwas took place over two sessions – the first being between him and me, marking the publication of the book *In Conversation: Samuel Wells and Stanley Hauerwas* (New York: Church Publishing, 2020). The second session involved two further conversation partners, Justin Coleman and Debra Dean Murphy, who know both his and my work well. Both conversations were moderated by Maureen Knudsen Langdoc, whose deft direction is invisible here.

I am immensely grateful to Jonathan Evens, Director of HeartEdge, to Andy Turner and to Ben Sheridan, whose curation of the programme made the whole enterprise possible. Rose Lyddon took over from Ben for the last two conversations. In many ways these published conversations reflect the internal dialogue we were having throughout the period about how HeartEdge could continue to reflect moods and set agendas in helpful and responsive ways. I am especially grateful to all the prophets, for offering their time and wisdom for no tangible reward and with such grace. Together they have renewed our discovery of what it means to be church, and what God has in store for us in the coming kingdom.

The Prophets

Walter Brueggemann is Professor Emeritus at Columbia Theological Seminary. He continues to write, most recently *Returning from the Abyss: A Study in Jeremiah*. He contributes regularly to the blog Church.Anew.

Steve Chalke is the founder of the Oasis Trust, which specializes in education, healthcare, supported housing and community development in the UK and various other countries. He is also an author, speaker, former UN Special Advisor on Human Trafficking and a Baptist minister.

Sarah Coakley is the Norris-Hulse Professor of Divinity, University of Cambridge, emerita, and now holds honorary positions at Australian Catholic University, University of St Andrews and Oriel College, Oxford. She continues to write her systematic theology, the second volume of which is entitled *Sin, Racism and Divine Darkness: An Essay 'On Human Nature'*.

Justin Coleman is Senior Pastor of University United Methodist Church in Chapel Hill, North Carolina, and a Consulting Faculty member at Duke Divinity School nearby. He is author of *Home for Christmas: Tales of Hope and Second Chances* and a contributor to *I'm Black, I'm Christian, I'm Methodist*.

Stephen Cottrell is the 98th Archbishop of York and a popular writer and speaker on evangelism, spirituality and catechesis, with a particular interest in retelling the Christian story imaginatively. His latest book, *Dear England*, addresses issues about how the Christian faith can shape the life of our nation.

Michael Curry is Presiding Bishop and Primate of The Episcopal Church. He was elected in 2015 to a nine-year term in this role, and the animating vision and message of his ministry is Jesus of Nazareth and his model of radical, sacrificial love.

Maggi Dawn is Professor of Theology, and Principal of St Mary's College, at Durham University. Prior to that, she was Associate Dean, and Professor of Theology and the Arts, at Yale University in the USA. Her first career was as a musician and songwriter. She is the author of five books, and numerous hymns and songs.

Kelly Brown Douglas is Dean of the Episcopal Divinity School and Bill and Judith Moyers Chair in Theology at Union Theological Seminary. Her academic work has focused on womanist theology, sexuality and the Black church, and racial and social justice. Her most recent book is *Resurrection Hope: A Future Where Black Lives Matter.*

Stanley Hauerwas is the Gilbert T. Rowe Professor Emeritus of Theological Ethics in the Divinity School of Duke University. He has also held the Chair in Theological Ethics at the University of Aberdeen. His most recent book is *Fully Alive: Karl Barth's Apocalyptic Humanism.*

John L. McKnight is Co-Founder of the Asset Based Community Development Institute and a Senior Associate of the Kettering Foundation. He has spent a lifetime assisting neighbourhoods to become the centre of society.

Chine McDonald was previously the head of public engagement at Christian Aid and is now director of Theos, the religion and society think tank. She is also vice-chair of Greenbelt Festival and a trustee of Christians in Media. Her second book is *God Is Not a White Man: And Other Revelations.*

Brian D. McLaren served as a pastor for over 20 years, during which time he began writing books. For the last 20 years, he has been an author, speaker, activist and networker. He teaches with the Center for Action and Contemplation. His most recent book is *Do I Stay Christian?*

Debra Dean Murphy is Professor of Religious Studies at West Virginia Wesleyan College where she also co-directs the Center for Restorative Justice. Her essay 'Becoming Grievable in Appalachia' appears in *Words for a Dying World: Stories of Grief and Courage from the Global Church*, edited by Hannah Malcolm (SCM Press).

Ben Quash is King's College London's first Professor of Christianity and the Arts. Prior to that, he was a Fellow of Fitzwilliam College and then of Peterhouse, Cambridge, and lecturer in the Faculty of Divinity in the University of Cambridge. He is General Editor of *The Visual Commentary on Scripture* (TheVCS.org).

Anthony Reddie is the Director of the Oxford Centre for Religion and Culture, Regent's Park College, University of Oxford. He is also a Professor Extraordinarius with the University of South Africa. He is a recipient of the Archbishop of Canterbury's Lanfranc Award for 2020 for services to Education and Scholarship.

Barbara Brown Taylor is a bestselling author, teacher and Episcopal priest. She has served on the faculties of colleges, universities and seminaries, but is most at home on a small farm in the foothills of the Appalachians that she shares with her husband Ed and their dogs, horses and other creatures.

Jonathan Tran holds the George W. Baines Chair of Religion at Baylor University in Waco, Texas, USA. His research explores the theological implications of the human life in language, especially focusing on the grammar of Christian speech.

Rachel Treweek is Bishop of Gloucester and Anglican Bishop for HM Prisons in England and Wales. She was consecrated as the 41st Bishop of Gloucester in 2015 and made history by becoming the first female diocesan bishop and the first female bishop in the House of Lords.

Samuel Wells is Vicar of St Martin-in-the-Fields in London, UK, and Visiting Professor of Christian Ethics at King's College London. His most recent book is *Humbler Faith, Bigger God*.

Lucy Winkett is Rector of St James's Church Piccadilly. A broadcaster and writer, she was among the first generations of women ordained in the Church of England. Her latest book *Reading the Bible with your Feet* was published by Canterbury Press in 2021. Lucy trained as a professional soprano before ordination.

Introduction

Christianity depends on a fundamental conviction that doesn't appear in the creeds and is impossible to prove. But it's simply put – there is another reality besides the one we're in – and it's in fact more real than the one we're in. I usually call that reality 'essence', and the one we're in 'existence'. But whatever you call it – heaven, the beyond, the spiritual – and whether you think it's up there, waiting to arrive here, or in some other realm entirely, it's suffused with God in a way this reality is not.

The crucial point about this other reality is that this existence doesn't make a whole lot of sense without it. We spend a lot of energy speculating on the mysteries of our existence. We wonder why there is suffering. We're confused and sometimes terrified at the fact that we die. We're perplexed that God is so eager to be in relationship with us but remains so out of reach. Meanwhile some urge us to be content with the universe as it is – big bang, evolution, natural selection and the circle of birth and death – and not seek more than that. But to different degrees, the answers to all these quandaries and ponderings lie in what I call essence – the reality beyond this one that's truer than this one. All our railing against God at what's wrong with the world, all our fury that this is such an imperfect existence – all of that matters much less if there's another reality that turns transitory life into eternal life, flawed relationships into fulfilled ones, fear and suspicion into trust and love.

Emmanuel Suhard was a complex man, a writer and priest who became Archbishop of Paris in 1940 and thereafter a cardinal. In his book *Priests Among Men*, he wrote some words that crystallize the importance of this conviction about another realm. He says:

> To be a witness does not consist in engaging in propaganda, nor even in stirring people up, but in being a living mystery. It means to live in such a way that one's life would not make sense if God did not exist.

Notice the two-edged character of this statement. It means a life that to most observers makes no sense. That means giving up the ways existence rewards lives that make a lot of sense – income, security, recognition, acclaim, awards, legacy. But it also means a life that in the light of God, in the time frame and perspective of essence, makes perfect sense. We could call it living God's future now.

The Old Testament isn't too interested in the word 'witness'. It has its own word for living a life that makes no sense if God does not exist. That word is 'prophet'. The prophet Samuel, from whom I get my own name, is a paradoxical figure. His ministry marks the great transition from Israel's hand-to-mouth occupation of the Promised Land, with a series of charismatic leaders known as judges, to a more ordered society under the leadership of a king. Eventually this also involved a transition from God's presence being embodied in the ark of the covenant, kept in a provisional tent, to its installation in the magnificent Jerusalem temple. The paradox is that Samuel wasn't at all sure these two celebrated transitions were such a good idea. And if we ponder Cardinal Suhard's words, we can understand why. Samuel saw that Israel was becoming like other nations – no longer directly dependent on the word of God but surrounded by institutions, procedures and traditions that made a whole lot of sense whether or not God existed. Today we would perhaps call them sustainability, or perhaps in America we'd call them democracy.

The First Book of Samuel begins with Hannah, who prays for a child and promises that, if she's given one, he will be given back to the Lord. When her wish is granted, she sings a beautiful song of what God has done, including these half-familiar words: '[The LORD] raises up the poor from the dust; he lifts the needy from the ash heap, to make them sit with princes and inherit a seat of honour.' Then we meet Samuel himself, as a boy, abiding in the shrine with Eli, the priest. What does all this remind you of? The whole story is reworked in the early chapters of the Gospels, where Mary sings of putting down the mighty from their seat and exalting the humble and meek, and where the boy Jesus is found in the temple talking with some teachers who look like updated versions of Eli. And then the penny drops. Who was the one who, above and beyond all others, lived in such a way that made no sense if God did not exist? At the risk of sounding like a caricature of a Sunday school class, the answer is Jesus.

And that gives us our definition of a prophet. A prophet is someone who lives in such a way that their life would not make sense if God did not exist; and, at the same time, a prophet points to Jesus. The classic portrayal of such a life and such a pointing is John the Baptist. The locusts and wild honey make no sense unless he's telling the world he's the promised Elijah who was expected to return before the Messiah appeared; and if you look at countless paintings of Jesus and John together, you'll invariably see John in some manner pointing to Jesus.

How do we go about becoming this kind of a prophet? I suggest there are three stages. The first is listening to God. For some people, contemplative prayer is life's centre – precisely where our lives make no sense if God does not exist. We simply listen. But that's not the only way to listen. Listening means studying wise commentary on world events, but also knowing when to put that commentary aside and listen to scripture, listen to God speaking in the mouths of those who don't conventionally get a hearing, listen to the wisdom of other centuries. The story of Samuel and Eli is about listening to a child. Being a prophet isn't firstly about what we say but who we listen to.

Then, second, it's about saying simple things. Everyone enjoys Hans Andersen's story of the emperor's new clothes. The emperor loved clothes. Two swindlers came to town, maintaining that their weaving was so fine that only those of refined taste could see it. His advisers feared to be thought fools, so no one pointed out that there was no cloth on the loom. Finally the swindlers declared the project complete. They persuaded the emperor to remove his clothes, and made the pretence that they were fitting him with the new ones. The emperor paraded through the city with no clothes, until a child pointed and said, 'He hasn't got anything on.' The whole city colluded in what today we call 'groupthink'. No one could see outside the deception they'd spun on each other. The child said the simple thing no one else was saying. The child was a prophet.

Then, third, it's about doing simple things, often things with wider reference. When Colin Kaepernick took a knee in September 2016 during the national anthem before a San Francisco 49ers American football game, he made the perfect prophetic gesture. Kaepernick was baptized Methodist, confirmed Lutheran and attends a Baptist church. Like Jesus riding a donkey rather than a horse into Jerusalem on Palm Sunday, it's absurd to receive it as a hostile statement. How could kneeling before flag and anthem be anything other than respectful of the values on which America believes itself to be founded? It's the fact that kneeling in submission is exactly what African Americans had to do as slaves for 300 years that makes the gesture prophetic and poignant. Taking the knee is an awesome gesture, because it says, 'You've made us subservient, despite the higher values you say our country is founded on. Now let's see those higher values.' Since the death of George Floyd four years later, now the whole world understands what it means to take a knee: to do a simple thing with wider significance. To be a prophet.

But here's the point about Colin Kaepernick. When he knelt in complaint, he was taking the devotional practice of personal prayer and making it a public statement of political protest. He was saying Christianity isn't simply about personal piety and individual salvation: it's about portraying a new society and organizing communities to advance that vision. And that's where the three dimensions of prophecy – choosing who to listen to, saying the thing no one's saying, and making gestures with wider significance – all come together. The way to change the world isn't to become a prophet. It's to join a prophetic community. You may be familiar with the words of the anthropologist Margaret Mead: 'Never doubt that a small group of thoughtful, committed citizens can change the world; indeed, it's the only thing that ever has.' But not everyone who hears those words joins such a community. Christians have a word for a community of prophetic action: we call it church. To be a church does not consist in engaging in propaganda, nor even in stirring people up, but in being a living mystery. It means to live in such a way that your life would not make sense if God did not exist.

For centuries we've built churches with spires. A spire is a way of pointing a finger to heaven – to remind people that there's another reality, more real than this one. The challenge for the church is to make its life as prophetic as its buildings. It's to listen, speak and act in ways that make no sense if God does not exist. And if we're short of ideas, we simply have Jesus, whose every gesture was a prophetic statement of another reality truer than this one. But let's not make the two mistakes embedded in the story of Samuel. Let's not imagine that our calling as a small group of thoughtful, committed, organized citizens is to be in charge: Samuel warned that the ministry of a prophet would be ruined by trying to become a king. And let's not suppose that one inspired prophet will do the job for us. It's not about raising up unique individuals; it's about becoming a prophetic community.

This book brings together a company of 17 prophets. What distinguishes each of them is who they are listening to, the things they say, and the things they do. When the HeartEdge movement sought a rapid way to respond to the pandemic and to capitalize on the online boom it evoked, I began to hold a series of live conversations on Zoom with figures in the public eye on both sides of the Atlantic who could point out the deeper theological and social realities of what we were experiencing together. What we were looking for was prophecy: guidance for living God's future now. This book contains the fruits of those conversations. Prophets don't point to themselves; they point to God. They reflect not just on our existence, but on God's essence. What follows are a series of 'spires': ways in which the finger of the church points to the wonder of heaven – in which influential figures describe what it means to live in such a way that one's life would not make sense if God did not exist.

Walter Brueggemann

Freedom

In a paper for the *Journal of Preachers* about pestilence and its place in the Old Testament, I talked about three kinds of pestilence: a transactional relationship between God in Israel where if Israel plays bad, God plays bad towards Israel; a mobilizing relationship where God uses the forces of creation to achieve a particular outcome; and the Job version of raw holiness, where you don't get to understand the ways of the raw and holy God. I think it's hazardous to make any connections to our own experience. But as I study the text, it seemed that those were three quite distinct ways of talking. The Old Testament text makes a big effort to see what happens if you draw pestilence into the world where God rules, which is what they tried to do. It's an obligation to think about the virus in the context of our faith. Obviously, all of these are pre-scientific ways of reasoning. And in the United States we're having a big argument about whether the government should pay any attention to science. I recognize the term pre-scientific; but it's not the same as anti-scientific.

I've been working on a follow-up to that to say that in the exile, the way the text presents it, God discovered new ways of compassion, about which God didn't know, until God saw that Israel was suffering so acutely. So there are not a lot of texts, but there are some texts that show God making a quite fresh move and taking a very fresh initiative as though to start over again. So I think the relationship is changed during the exile. One can see the same thing about the flood narrative in Genesis, that what really changes the narrative is God's inclination toward creation. Nothing changes about creation. But God is at a new place in treating with creation.

The Old Testament doesn't articulate God in ontological terms, but in dramatic terms, so God is a player in an ongoing drama. If God is a real player, then God has to have the kind of freedom that every actor has in a drama, to develop role and character. And I think that's what happens. The pivotal text for that argument is Hosea 11. God is very angry at Israel, and then right in the middle of the poem, God has a breadth of insight that says, 'I don't want it that way any more.' And every parent knows about that. Every parent knows about the discovery in the middle of all that: a very different impulse. The prophetic poets of Israel home in on the emergence of that surprising impulse, which in the literature happens over and over; but no doubt the exile is the primary place where that happens.

I wouldn't use the word progression or development, I would just use the word freedom. It's not linear, getting better and better. But it is the freedom to take new initiatives of self-presentation and self-articulation. And if you do that, then it's easy to see that in Jesus of Nazareth, God takes yet another fresh initiative that we had not witnessed before. To my mind that's very different from the old liberal notion of progression that has, within it, supersessionism: that in Jesus, we've gone beyond Jewishness. We left the Jews behind.

In the ongoing interpretive tradition of the church we get fresh disclosures or fresh insights, or fresh revelations that are evoked by particular historical circumstances. One doesn't have to argue that those are completely new; but they are fresh, different alternatives. So if you take Luther, for example, his radical articulation of the grace of God represents something of a new moment in our capacity to discern God. That doesn't mean that it's not older in the tradition, but it means it's a fresh articulation. And I think that your [Sam Wells'] work on improvisation was another kind of summons to freedom and imagination – a decisive moment in our ongoing understanding about this relationship with God that had never been seen quite that way before.

I'm talking about two possible ways to understand the Covid-19 virus. The first way is as a time to come to a newer understanding of ourselves: ourselves in relationship to creation, ourselves in relationship to God. The second is a way of understanding God's freedom. Like most of us, I am more comfortable with the first. That is, that the virus is a summons for us to rethink what it is we are about and hopefully to be inching towards some new notions of what's normal. Beijing has clean air for the first time without so much pollution. Kids are not getting so sick, because they're not going to school to pass sicknesses around. So this is an opportunity to re-examine how we have organized our common life as mainly the pursuit of commodities. What we are discovering, in our quarantines, is that relationships count more than commodities. Maybe this is a chance to completely reorient the administration of commodities in our economy. In relation to the second approach, the elemental covenantal attributes of God – justice and compassion and mercy and faithfulness – more sharply define what it means to be human. Now, that may not be a great crisis in Britain, but in the United States we have long since forgotten that those ways of being human are remote from the dominant ideologies of our society. So I call that in some ways freshly revelatory, even though it's been in front of us all the time.

Then the question is, what is the virus showing us about God? I think it shows us that God can be absent. So I've been working on the whole notion of God forsaking us. We are not really godforsaken – but we *feel* godforsaken. And when we feel God has forsaken us, we have to entertain the thought that we are in the moment godforsaken – the way in which Israel, in the exile, was indeed godforsaken. I'm working on that text in Isaiah 54.7, where God says, 'For a moment, I did forsake you.' I've been thinking about how long a moment is. And it turned out to be a very long time.

But, of course, Isaiah 54 comes immediately after Isaiah 53. Isaiah didn't just peel the whole thing off from 1 to 66. It's a bit of a hotchpotch. I don't think that's a disgraceful thing to say, although it's not a scholarly term. But leaving that aside, if you take a canonical view, we read it as 53, followed by 54. Isaiah 53 is, for Christians, one of the most significant texts in the Old Testament, and it gives us a picture of a God who responds to suffering, possibly even pestilence, by taking that suffering into God's own person and body.

The pandemic is a wake-up call for how we do theology. So much theology is abstract and remote, and lacking in imagination. Good theology has to resist generalizations and always stick with the specificity of the narrative. So the Bible is essentially a collage of specific articulations. And then we arrange them: it's almost like a Rorschach test. We arrange them to arrive at some place where we think we can live for a while. They are just tugging at our identity and our imagination. We are always arriving at a new articulation of who we are and how we want to be. It's a very open process. Every time you get up to preach, you reconfigure it all in a fresh way.

What does relationship without touch mean? And what does this ambiguous kind of presence mean? Obviously touch is very important to relationality. But it's much thicker than that. And it has many other dimensions of seeing and hearing and remembering and hoping. Many people are going to retirement homes and nursing homes and touching the window of their loved ones. But there's a glass between their hands, right, they imagine touching each other; and so we do all that. We are learning again how to do relationship. And that turns out to be so much more interesting and so much more important than simply acquiring more consumer commodities. In some ways that's the great debate in the United States about when we open up the economy. It's really an argument about the relative importance of relationships and commodities. Meanwhile our president[1] has no capacity for relationship at all. So he represents the extreme articulation that life consists in commodities – which may sound like a strange replay of Margaret Thatcher about market and society in some ways.

The godforsaken texts in the Old Testament are written with the conviction of homecoming and restoration, just as in and with the cross, there is always Easter. Biblical honesty is always in the presence of biblical hope. So it's not just honesty: that would be a cul de sac. It's always towards some kind of new well-being.

But when Israel came back from exile it was not the same. It's not the same in good ways, it's not the same in bad ways. While Judaism after the exile was multifaceted, there were the ambitions of a restored monarchy, or restored temple, but they were not the dominant tradition. There was a real shifting of gears away from temple, away from monarchy, to Torah teaching. If you factor that out, logically, you would say that restoration in the United States is not the ambition of being the dominant military superpower in the world. But maybe there are other trajectories that need to command our restored sense of identity and will do, because there's got to be a great pressure to recover all of that. The temple represents a quest for certitude. The monarchy represents a quest for domination. And I think it is up to people who are grounded in the Torah tradition, like us, to make the case that neither certitude nor domination overshadow the kingdom of God. So the question is whether we have the resources and the courage and the imagination to articulate alternative notions of normalcy that can enter into the political conversation.

If our prayer life with God is an actual transaction, with someone who is on the other end of the transaction, then we have an obligation to insist that God must embrace God's best self, which is an odd way to talk. But then we urge that the government must embrace its best self, and so on. So it is a summons to reconsider, reposition, redefine and recharacterize. And I think that's going to be our work.

In the United States that work goes on to mean a redistribution of our commonwealth, tax policy and all the things that are related to that. And that requires organizing to mobilize political energy. Acts of neighbourly charity are important. But we are tempted to think that acts of neighbourly charity are enough. Yet we really need to address the common good of the political enterprise. That's a Christian thing to be worried about. It strikes me as a paradox. If you listen to some of the more thoughtful broadcasts, people are saying, this is such an interesting moment where government is having to reflect on what the common

---

1 At the time of this conversation, Donald Trump was US President.

good is and how that balances between health and wealth, or medical issues or economics. And I always want to say at the end of that, isn't that what government is always? It's about balancing these different interests. You're obviously much further along in Britain than we are about those matters. It's very much in our news, that some public person in Britain said that the healthcare programme is the new Anglican Church. We have no parallel to that at all.

By his narrative engagement with particular persons, Jesus critiqued the entire system, and led people to imagine an alternative way of being society, which I suppose is what got him executed. But I have no doubt that's what his ministry is about. He contrasts the kingdom of God with the kingdom of Rome, which was essentially predatory. All his actions are actions of resistance, and alternative.

We in the United States have to move beyond our treasured notion of exceptionalism to see that we are a member of the international community, and with our great resources we have responsibility in the international community. And you may have noticed that what has happened in the United States is that there are different states who have been willing to share ventilators with other states. So it can be done, and on larger scale we obviously need to think the same way about the resources that developed countries have in hand, and what that means for all of us who are in this together. That's very un-American thinking, but very urgent.

While the main claim of the Old Testament is that Israel is God's chosen people, there is also in the Old Testament an uneasiness with that, and an awareness that the God who chose Israel has also chosen many other peoples. The notion of being the chosen people is an acute one in the United States and it has to be vigorously combated, to show that God chooses many people. There are many chosen peoples, and we have no particular advantage. So that requires a very different self-understanding and very vigorous teaching. And some of that has to do with white people being the chosen people, Western people asserting all our privileges and our entitlements.

There is an extraordinary passage in Isaiah 19.24, where God says:

On that day Israel will be the third with Egypt and Assyria, a blessing in the midst of the earth, whom the LORD of hosts has blessed, saying, 'Blessed be Egypt my people, and Assyria the work of my hands, and Israel my heritage.'

So God identifies three chosen peoples. Micah 4.5 adds a verse that says, 'For all the peoples walk, each in the name of its god, but we will walk in the name of the LORD our God for ever and ever', which is a recognition of incredible pluralism.

I have a very vigorous conviction that the God of life will prevail. And I have a very minimal conviction about everything else. So my standard certitude is that my death will not interrupt God's being. And God will continue to be the God of mercy, justice and compassion, and all that good stuff. And I don't think much more than that. So my destiny, however that is, will leave me knowing about the God of mercy. As for whether I will go into a second edition, I have no idea about that. I don't think about that. I don't worry about it.

When people look back on the pandemic in 50 years' time, I think they would say we began to realize our proper position. That combats both our enormous pride and our compelling despair. Lively interaction as covenant permits us to resist both pride and despair. We have a chance of seeing that clearly in this crisis.

14 May 2020

2

John McKnight

Friendship

An asset-based approach is one that says if we want, at a neighbourhood level, to do something, there are three steps to doing it. And it's important that these three steps be sequential. You can't take one of them alone. And you can't start with the third step. You must start with the first one.

The first step is to ask, if we understand all of the capacities and gifts and assets in our neighbourhood, what can we do with them? If we're trying to achieve anything, the first question is, what can we do with the resources that we have? The second question is, what assistance from some outside institution do we need in order to enable us to continue to be effective? And the last question is, where can we turn when we find that we can't achieve what we want to achieve with what we have, even with some help from outside? We can't do it at all. The way to know what it is that an outside system or institution really should be doing is to have gone through the first two steps.

In other words, if you start with the question, 'What is it that only outside institutions can do?' then you never get to the citizen-acting part of the first question. Asset-based community development (ABCD) says that the residual resource is institutional capacities and inputs. But you'll never know what you need from those kinds of institutions until you go through the first two steps.

Something happened to me some years ago. I always lived in an apartment building and hadn't yet enough money to buy a house. I had always wanted a garden, so when I had one I immediately planted half the back-yard. Then I went away to Toronto for a month to be a part of a faculty there. I came back one evening, and next morning I went to my office. Coming back, I stopped at a grocery store and shopped for fresh vegetables. I brought them home and put them on the counter and my wife said to me, 'Go out and look in your backyard.' So I went and looked and I had 14 tomato plants dripping with tomatoes. I had cabbage, lettuce, onions, green peppers. I felt pretty sheepish. But I had been away for a month, so I didn't realize that everything was there. My wife smiled at me, and said, 'You'll never know what you need, until you know what you have.'

That's what the ABCD process leads you to: what do I have? Then, what do I need? But never start with the question, 'What do I need from out there?' So at any time, that's the process that we focus on. Now, in the current situation of states in the US where we're having uprisings every place, there's quite a demand for doing something different about the police. Some people are calling for us to do away with the police. Or defund them. But an ABCD approach would say neighbourhoods can perform all kinds of functions. One of those functions is to take on responsibility for our safety and security. What resources do we have that would allow us to be the producers of our safety and security? Second, what do we need to help us be better at doing what we could do with our own resources? What's out there that can be supportive? And then we'll know the answer to the question, 'Do we really need police?' The answer may be, actually we do need police. We don't need people who are called police. And we don't need people who do what police do. But we need people from the outside who can do some of the things we can't do. But we start with *what we can do*. And that's going on in a lot of places.

Real community development is based on thinking about functions rather than programmes. We have a list of seven functions that neighbourhoods are peculiarly able to take on, and do better than institutions. They include things like safety, health, environment or ecology, security, food, the care of children. If the resources that are available in local neighbourhoods to perform those functions are mobilized, they're more significant than what institutions can do in that domain. As an example in the health area, if you ask what are the determinants of health in a neighbourhood, the least important of the five major determinants is access to medical care. So if you really wanted to be healthy, you'd have to ask what are we doing about our individual behaviour, about our group behaviour, about the physical environment, and about our income – because all four of those have much more to do with health than access to medical care. In rural areas where you have low per capita doctors to the population of patients, compared to places where there's a high relationship between the number of doctors and the number of people per capita, there's almost no difference in health.

The per capita presence of doctors is not a major factor in terms of our health. I don't want to do away with them. But doctors are not in the centre of the conversation. So ABCD people would never say, 'We are concerned about what institutions do.' That's our last concern, because we have to make sure that the functions we can do with what we have are enabled and activated first. Otherwise, we're going to end up being nothing but sad little consumers and clients in a big system.

We have an ABCD faculty, which is about 50 people distributed all over North America. Only one or two are in a university, but we call them the faculty. Each of them is manifesting an ABCD approach to the issues or concerns of the people in the neighbourhoods where they are. And we have a collective learning on the basis of that kind of experience.

The two most important assets by far are the gifts and the capacities of the local residents, and the clubs, groups, organizations and associations that they put together in all kinds of permutations, which are the way they become more powerful. An individual's gift shared with six other people and their gifts is the ultimate source of community power. We call that an association. And there are all kinds of them. If I were a pastor, one way of thinking about it is, in this neighbourhood I am surrounded by people, full of gifts, capacities, skills, abilities and knowledge, all ungiven, all unshared: they're waiting to give it or share it. The question is, what has to happen for that revelation of capacity to come forward? A lot of our on-the-ground work involves people on a block; a person starts out by going door to door and asking people who live in each household, 'Can you tell us what you have that you value – that is so significant to you that you think you could share it with the other people on the block?' So many people have done this.

Let me describe questions we would tend to use. The first question is, what are your gifts? Gifts are what you're born with, rather than what you learn. The second is, what are your skills and abilities? That means things that you've learned. Third, what are your passions? What do you care enough about, with such intensity, that you've acted on it? And the fourth is, what do you know well enough that you could share or teach it with or to other adults or young people in this neighbourhood?

We know that if somebody who's a neighbour goes and talks to the next-door neighbour and asks those four questions – or you could add other ones – you'll find people will give you on average four responses to each. So you've got 16 things that have special significance to that person. Then we ask, would you be willing to share these things? And over 90 per cent of people will say yes to that. So now think about the street next to your church. Say there are 30 households on this street. I know that there's at least one person in each household, and there are probably more – I'm thinking here about adults – but let's just say one and, on average, they're going to give me 16 assets, or capacities they have that they're willing to share with their neighbours. So if each household has 16 gifts to share, and there are 30 households, the total number of assets comes to 480.

So, pastor, go out and look in your garden. There are 480 gifts waiting to be given. Now what can you do that would enable all that potential to contribute? If I were a pastor, I would think my best activity is to activate the visibility of the gifts that surround me. That's true in the church itself. But it's also true in the neighbourhood. And a similar thing is true of the clubs, groups and associations. So the last question the neighbour asks is, can you tell me any of the groups, clubs, organizations and associations you belong to? In the US, the answer to that, on average, is five. So if we have 30 households with five associations, then five times 30 is 150 associations. So, pastor, the other thing you're surrounded with are tens and twenties and fifties and hundreds of associations. And they tend to be invisible. So maybe the task is to ask how we can act in ways that make visible the invisible riches of gifts and associations that surround us. We would call that ABCD organizing.

The symbol we've always used is a glass where the water goes up to the middle. So the glass is half empty and half full. People who are focused on needs start with the empty half. People who are focused on assets start with the full half. Everything I've been describing is about how you identify the full half. However, Saul Alinsky's type of organizing, and a lot of organizing, doesn't start with the full half. It starts with the empty half. I spent 20 years doing this, so I'm not arguing against it. I'm trying to make a distinction that is important in terms of being effective. But when I'm thinking from a full-half perspective, I call the empty-half issues. And what I mean by issues is that, in our neighbourhood, the city picks up the garbage half as often as it does in the rich neighbourhoods. Therefore, in our neighbourhood, we have rats, and in richer neighbourhoods they don't. That's an issue. Now, the way we're going to organize people as a community organizer is to find how many people are concerned enough about that issue that they're willing to act on it. And so if I'm the organizer, and I'm interviewing a person on board doing what we call one on one, I'm trying to find out which of the issues (or the empty half) the person is angriest about. Why am I interested in anger? Because that's a great mobilization test, very likely to get that person to come out and be part of our organization to change things. If I can build the organization around something that they have the motive to act on, I'm looking for issues they'll act on.

And then what we'll do – I remember doing this myself – is get a bunch of maybe 20 or 30 rats. We'll gather everybody who is really concerned about rats and we'll hire a bus – maybe we can get 40 people on the bus – and we'll go down to City Hall with our rats. We'll walk in as normal. We'll take the lift up to the fifth floor where the mayor's office is, and we'll walk very nicely to the door of the mayor's office and open it; and probably somebody there will ask us what we're doing. And we'll say the mayor doesn't do the job that he or she should do. We're a rat-infested neighbourhood because the mayor is incompetent, so we thought we should share the rats with the mayor. And we open the rat traps and let the rats out in the mayor's office. Probably the next day, the ward committeeman will be out there with the sanitation workers doing something about the garbage and the rats.

So I have started with a need, a problem or a deficiency. I have organized people around their anger about that need. And that has mobilized them to confront the institution called city government. And they come and they do what I want them to do. That's so much fun. I love doing that kind of stuff. However, I am always acting collectively as a consumer. I'm not doing anything about rats. That whole process embodies the idea that I am a consumer.

And it's necessary in circumstances that people do that. But you're never really powerful as a consumer. Your real power is as a producer. Most issue-oriented organizing always keeps you as a consumer. What ABCD adds to you is your ability to be a producer. That's the difference. Any neighbourhood group ought to have both powers. We try to work with neighbourhood groups in that way.

Because we are so local in our focus, we can be committed to face-to-face and relationship, rather than electronic engagement. The electronic world, the world of screens, whether it's television or internet, if you take whatever benefits they provide against the negative effects, in my mind there's no question that they have mainly produced a new set of negative effects that we didn't have in the past. I was 26 years old before I ever saw something called a television in the house. (I was 50 before I ever saw something called a computer.) With no electronic screen within sight, people often ask me, what did you do with your time? Let me ask you, how much of your life is sitting in front of the screen? Is it three hours? Eight hours? Ten hours? Well, I don't have any of those hours. So my entire upbringing was incapacitated because I didn't have screens. I'm saying that facetiously. I think that the greatest benefit I had in the formation of my life was that I had no screens. I had people. When I came home from school, I didn't have an iPhone to fiddle with, or a television to watch. And so like every child in the whole world, I went outside and joined with other children and created a life. I think human creativity is fading out. Marshall McLuhan said the media is the message. There's not a message in the media, the media is the message.

Ivan Illich and I used to talk about the fact that society throughout all time until very recently was an entity that lived on land. The electronic world that now consumes a third of all our time has created a great breaking point with whatever space is the real space. I walk my dog all the time, I live in a neighbourhood where everybody has a porch. I never see anybody on the porch. If we were on the porch, we'd probably begin to be something like a community, but we're not on the porch. The environment is a screen, and we're inside. It's taking us out of a world where relationships with each other are the framework of life. A lot of young people, if they talk about something, talk about something they see on the internet. But supposing I took it away. What would they talk about? Well, they might create something. When I was a kid, I created something every day with my fellow young people. There is a difference between a world where the environment is people and the world where the environment is an electric screen. I am nostalgic for not having electric screens consume a third of the lives of most of the people in the country I live in. I think it's a net loss, which individualizes and makes people ever more powerless. But the one thing that I have seen that is enabling about the internet is its possibility to get people who would not otherwise come face to face in mutual activity together. And in lockdown that's been literally a lifesaver for the neighbourhoods.

I'm no theologian, but I've always been closely wedded to one text of the New Testament. And it is Jesus having the Last Supper. He knows what's ahead. And he's deciding to tell these people who were there with him, and had been empowered, what's the most important thing. He says, 'I no longer call you servants. I call you friends.' Few people who are Christians have heard that message. Christian service is a great mistake. He told us at the end, I don't call you servants. So I'm not saying, be a public servant. I say, be a friend. The power of friendship is the mutuality of gifts and the recognition of joint fallibility. To me, ABCD is a way of saying, if you are a gift-minded person, then you are always in the land of giftedness and friendship. Towards the end of his life, Jesus says it all comes down to friendship. And I must say of all the Christian groups that I've been associated with, the one I think is the best is the Society of Friends because they're not about service – they're friends. They got their name right. The challenge is, how do we move from service to friendship? The key to unlocking that door is to be gift-oriented rather than needs-oriented.

11 June 2020

3

Chine McDonald

Dignity

A few years ago, I sat with a friend over brunch, and she said to me, 'Let's do our mission statements. What's God saying to you?' I articulated that I wanted to commit my life to communicating the good news of Christianity to a world that no longer necessarily understood it or found it an accessible concept. At that point, I was working for a Christian organization, and I realized that we weren't always being seen as good news in the world. I wanted to work for an organization that I could see was doing tangible good in the world, so I moved into international development, first for World Vision and then for Christian Aid.

The reason why I love working for Christian Aid is because it's not just about feeding people or meeting people's immediate needs, although we do those things during humanitarian crises. Christian Aid is about trying to tackle the systematic inequalities that keep people in poverty or put people in poverty in the first place. We don't just talk about the small issues but also about the big picture of our economic global economic system. What are the things that need to be changed in order to create a fairer and more equal world? That's our core mission: to stand for dignity, equality and justice for all people.

Christian Aid is often at government tables. We have meetings at the World Bank, big meetings with powerful people. But I think it's often more impactful to stand outside those centres of power and look at what governments are doing; to be able, as an outsider, to push the governments to do certain things and to praise governments when they're doing things that benefit the poorest and most marginalized communities in the world. As part of a governmental body, you're less free to do those things. I prefer to be an agitator in that space rather than being part of a governmental organization.

There is a huge question about what it means to be a postcolonial aid agency – to avoid replicating the same mindsets that pervaded the colonial era. It's a question that we at Christian Aid – and a lot of NGOs in the UK – are currently wrestling with. I was born in Nigeria, in Lagos, but I'm from the Ebo tribe: the Biafran tribe that tried to break away from Nigeria in the 1960s. This January, we celebrated 50 years since the end of the Biafran war. So, I think I bring a different perspective from someone who is white and British-born. My dad often talks about how he dreads the day when he sees a picture of himself in an archive photo from the Biafran war with a big belly or flies around his face, because that was his reality. That was my parents' reality. So when I see images in our fundraising materials, it's easier for me than it might be for white people to understand those people as people who could be my family.

That said, I work in fundraising and communications. I know how easy it can be to replicate colonial narratives about benevolent donors who are white British people, helping the poor Africans who can't help themselves. I also know that my parents are thankful for the help that was received from members of the British public who were moved to give all those years ago during the Biafran war. But there is a shame that comes with that for first- and second-generation immigrants who want to combat the stereotype that African people – or people from the Global South – are entirely helpless.

Organizations like Christian Aid have staff around the world who are literally walking alongside the communities we work with – who are themselves members of those communities. It's not necessarily us here and them over there. It's us *with*. What we do in the UK is to tell the story of those living in desperate, horrendous situations around the world, and enable British people to be generous and have empathy with the plight of other people. We at Christian Aid have gone through quite a lot of change over the past couple of years. Our CEO, Amanda Mukwashi, is of Zambian origin, and she has really challenged us in the way that we think and the words that we use about the communities we work with. We used to talk about 'beneficiaries', but we've moved away from language like that – language that suggests a one-way relationship.

We talk about every one of us – me and people in the communities that we work with – being made in God's image. That means they have as much dignity as I do, and they should be treated with dignity. Our mission is not to work for them, but to work alongside them for equality and justice. To me it is a manifestation of the incarnation – God being with us in times of suffering. When I studied theology at the University of Cambridge, I focused a lot on the sociology and anthropology of religion. One of my main interests was the concept of gift exchange – whether a gift can be freely given or whether the giver always benefits from it. I often think about that in relation to our work – whether it matters that a British person giving £50 to Christian Aid is giving selflessly or whether they derive a bit of joy, or a sense of power and, either way, a warm, fuzzy feeling, because they're helping others who are less fortunate.

I also try to think about the systemic and structural changes that need to be made. You could see that as addressing the imbalance on the scales. My mind has been changed even over the past few weeks as I've been reading about the history of Africa, pre-transatlantic slave trade. Even as an African person, I have fallen into the narrative of thinking that African people are subservient, oppressed losers in the global game. Educating myself about the stories of Africa, the creativity of Africa, the inner intellect of Africa, the victories of Africans, has allowed a real change in mindset for me. Even in the context of the slave trade, hearing stories of Africans who fought from the shore against slave ships, who rebelled on slave ships, has the power to shift the narrative. I'd never heard those stories before. Thinking about Christianity in fourth-century Ethiopia helped me think about Africa differently. Once you have a fairer understanding of what Africa as a continent is, it becomes less about scarcity and abundance, and more about justice, equality and fairness.

There's not a group of us talking in London and then disseminating messages to our colleagues in Bangladesh or Africa. It's much more of a conversation that we can have on an equal level. I've observed some really interesting things. Christian Aid week happened in May (2020), which was obviously bad timing for our biggest fundraiser of the year. But we were amazed to see how our supporters were really creative and innovative with their fundraising. We raised more money than we thought we were going to. At the start of the pandemic, we were thinking if the UK is being affected like this, then imagine what's going to happen in Africa, in Southeast Asia, in South Asia: they're really going to struggle. But the doom that was predicted for those countries that we see as less able to help themselves has not happened. In fact, some of the powerful countries in the world, the US and the UK, have been affected much more than the countries we work in. What does that teach us? Why aren't we hearing about that a lot? Why aren't we celebrating African success on coronavirus and the creativity that has happened? They went into lockdown much earlier. We don't talk about it because there's a patronizing view of Africa. It must have been an accident, and they haven't experienced it; or it must be because they have a younger demographic. That's a lesson about pride, hubris, assuming that we have the answers and they do not, and we must help them. I'm glad that it hasn't yet been catastrophic in those countries. But we need to be careful about the assumptions that we make.

Words like systemic and structural move our focus from small, individual acts to the whole infrastructure that shapes people's lives. Let's talk about white privilege, for example – which is a term that's been bandied around a lot and at which some people take offence. I can totally understand how a poor person living in north-east England, who is white, might say, 'Well, I haven't got any privilege.' But that's not necessarily the point. Privilege doesn't mean that your life is perfect or amazing. It means there are certain systems – things that are bigger than the individual – that mean Black people, as a community, are less able to do certain things or access certain opportunities. Those are fundamental things that need to change. The Archbishop of Canterbury talked about structural racism within the Church of England. We're not talking about someone using the wrong word to describe a Black person in a meeting. We're not talking about an individual saying a racist thing to another person. We're talking about the stories that we tell ourselves as the Church of England as a whole – about the way that we appoint within the Church of England, the way we do interviews, the ways we allocate funding, the kinds of people who hold positions of power. How does that perpetuate certain inequalities within the church? It's not about the individual, it's about the bigger structures and systems.

I have only seen the George Floyd video once. I'm not sure I could watch it again. It was 8 minutes and 46 seconds that the police officer knelt on his neck. That is such a long time. That is such a long time to be kneeling on someone while they are shouting for their mother, while they're saying, 'I can't breathe'. What does that say about the respective positions those people have in the world? Or the eyes that are watching it happen? What do they think about those people? I also have been thinking about the police officers who were around who didn't kneel on his neck. Why didn't they stop him? I've been trying to understand how I could be watching my colleagues do that and not say anything – complicity, what it means not to be the person who does the bad thing, but to be silent in the face of injustice. Either you agree and you think that that's an okay thing to do, which would explain why you might not say stop, or you're scared, or you don't know what to do. So you do nothing. I wonder if that's a symbol of the predominantly white church in the Western world.

The reason why I've only watched the video once is because it was extremely traumatic. It continues to be traumatic for everyone who watches it – but particularly for Black people. There's something about being part of the Black community – we are intensely communal. In a lot of African tribes or traditions, your victory is my victory. Your death is my death. When a lot of Black people are looking at George Floyd, they're also seeing themselves. They're also seeing their own necks on the line. It's been described as vicarious trauma. While I was watching

George Floyd, I was thinking about the trauma of the brutalization of black bodies that I have watched all my life, not just in police brutality, but throughout my childhood in reading about the civil rights movement or watching media like *Roots*. It lets you know how you're seen by the world. For a lot of successful Black people for whom it might seem that life is going pretty well, watching that footage was a reminder of how Black people are seen, inevitably, whether they're doing well or not.

I've written a book called *God is Not a White Man*. The real point of the book is not just that God is not a white man, but that white men are not gods. We talk about the *imago Dei*, and all of us are talking about black death, black trauma, perceptions of Africa and so on. I think it's obvious that there's something wonderful in creating God in our image – or in art that depicts God as like us – because that is the incarnation. In the incarnation God comes to earth as a man – not a white man with a long beard and blue eyes, but as a Middle Eastern Jew.

It makes sense that white people imagine God looking like them. My problem is that, when I think about Jesus, that's what I see as well. That's what my mum sees when she thinks about Jesus. That's what my grandmother, who lives in Nigeria, sees. The problem is the crossover into cultures where there's no one who looks like that. When there's no one that looks like that, how can you relate in the same way to Christ coming for your salvation? It creates a distance when thinking about our own salvation. It makes us feel lesser. We fall into a narrative that says the most perfect human is a white man – and therefore, I am not the perfect version of a human. I'm less than, not only because I'm not white, but also because I'm a woman. The fact that Black people, African people, or people in the Global South picture Jesus as a white man with blue eyes is an illustration of how pervasive white supremacy is around the world.

I'm very proud that my great-grandfather was an Anglican priest in south-east Nigeria. He ran a church in the village – what some people would call the bush. Women used to come to my great-grandmother before they were getting married, to stay with her for a while and prepare to be good Christian wives. They learned how to drink tea out of china cups, how to bake cakes, how to set the table – because Christianity was, at that point, synonymous with Englishness and whiteness. When you became a Christian, in order to be a good Christian, you had to be as close to whiteness and Englishness as possible. I wonder how that distorts your faith, looking at Christianity through that lens.

I am learning to understand the gospel as the opposite of that. I've been reading James Cone's *The Cross and the Lynching Tree*, which is devastating and beautiful. The lynching is a symbol for the crucifixion: Christ on the cross is with us in our suffering, with those who suffer at the hands of oppressors. It completely subverts the perception of Christianity as a religion that upholds power. It's the opposite of all those things that I see illustrated in white American evangelicalism at the moment. There's something in the Black Lives Matter movement – and in all our discussions about racial justice in recent months – that gets to the heart of what the Christian faith is actually about. I was in a meeting a couple of weeks ago, where someone said something quite controversial that I found difficult to hear. They said that you could not be a white Christian – because your whiteness, your power, always comes before your Christianity. Obviously, I don't believe that Christianity is just for Black people, but he was making the point that it's easier for a camel to go through the eye of a needle than for a white person to enter the kingdom of God. As Christians, we have to be willing to let go of our power. Christ is always with the oppressed and the marginalized and the people without the power. Unfortunately, that's often in conflict with how the Christian faith is practised, particularly in the West.

I'm really excited by this moment, even though I'm finding it traumatic at times. Christian leaders are thinking about these things and speaking out. Some Christians (though by no means all) are wrestling with these issues deeply. This is an opportunity to do some deep thinking and learning about what we understand by the Christian faith and about our place within the church and the world. The civil rights movement of the 1960s was powered by individuals within the church. The church has often been right at the heart of our cry for racial justice and justice in all its forms, all over the world. The church is also part of the Black Lives Matter movement. We're not necessarily leading it, but we are right there. We can walk alongside those who are on this journey – supporting, speaking out, doing practical things within our own churches, within our communities, to join with those who are calling for justice. We can break down the structures of oppression wherever we find them. We can let go of our power.

It's important that there are commentators who are Black, like me, who are being called to speak out. But it's also important for white people to have these conversations by themselves. There are some uncomfortable things that need to be brought to the surface and talked through. I wouldn't necessarily like to be in those rooms, but it's important to have those conversations and not look to Black people to fix everything. Because it's not our problem. We didn't start it and we haven't perpetuated it.

We need to celebrate our difference. We are all different and all of us are made in the image of God: our diversity comes from God and tells us something about what God is like. The issue is when difference is cast out, oppressed, put in certain boxes or forced to conform to stereotypes.

Part of the problem of white supremacy is that it has created these two categories of black and white; it has obscured how different we all are as individuals. Racial justice means tearing down those categories and celebrating the fact that we are all different – all uniquely made in the image of God.

9 July 2020

Chine McDonald is now Director of Theos. Patrick Watt took over from Amanda Mukwashi as Christian Aid's CEO in May 2022.

4

Rachel Treweek

Speech

As I look back on the path that has led me to where I am now, I realize that my driving passion is all about relationship, connection, communication: finding a voice. At the age of 14, I wanted to be a speech and language therapist. One of the people who really helped me find my voice – and I wish I'd let her know this before she died – was called Grace Wyatt. Grace set up a nursery called Charnwood, which was the first preschool nursery for families with disabled children. As a young person, I went and helped to run some holiday clubs with her in Stockport. What inspired me was her passion for living God's justice: seeing everyone as equal and valued, helping them to inhabit the kingdom, helping each person to find their unique voice.

My role as Bishop of Gloucester gives me authority to speak and responsibility to take up that authority. I often reflect on the fact that when I speak as 'Rachel, Bishop of Gloucester', people sometimes pay attention to things I was saying before I was a Bishop when people didn't seem so interested.

When I was a teenager and was given responsibilities in school, I would think, 'Well, I'm not sure I can do that.' But someone believed in me, so I dared to have a go. I try to remember that when I think about how to take up authority in my role. How do I communicate to every person that they are equally valuable, unique and precious? How do I give them confidence to be who they are called to be and take up the roles they are called to at that particular time? We often have different roles that we are given at particular times in our lives. We shouldn't push aside that authority, but rather accept that this is where God has called us in this moment, and in taking up that authority we have to take risks. I've learned that if you never dare to take risks, if you never speak out and get something wrong, you will never grow and you will never enable other people to flourish in the same way.

Given some of the failings of the church it can sometimes be challenging for bishops to speak with authority. As you explore the halls of power and authority, how can you speak into that space without your voice becoming distorted? It starts with the risk of admitting that we are broken, flawed human beings. The vision of the kingdom of God requires me to speak out for peace and justice and mercy and love – and to know that I will sometimes get it wrong. It asks us to remember the humility of Christ: how Jesus emptied himself and still knew who he was. Jesus, knowing where he was from, knowing his calling, then chose to get up, tie the towel around his waist and wash the disciples' feet. I draw on that a lot in my role – confidence that God has called me to this time and this place, tempered by humility. I have been called to this role and I need to have the courage to stand up, and then to kneel. It's about how you hold together that humility, that servant heart, without pushing away your authority because you think power is a dirty word. I need to take up authority *with* humility – and, unlike Christ, I will often get it wrong. Someone once said to me that the sin is not in the falling down, it's in the failing to get up. I've found that helpful throughout my life: take risks, fall over, but get up again – because there's always hope.

Occupying a position of authority is not about being better than someone else. It's about being able to sit with someone as an equal and say, 'I am Rachel, I am a flawed human being, but I'm also your bishop. And in that role, this is the authority I need to exercise.' Our different roles don't diminish our equality. There are broken processes like the Clergy Discipline Measure, which I have to work within even though they are hugely flawed. The way those processes can make people feel like they are on unequal ground can keep me awake at night and it can be extremely lonely to ultimately have to make those calls alone. I try to hold in mind, as I'm in conversations with people, that it's about their well-being, the well-being of the church, and the well-being of communities. But I don't always feel I get that completely right for everyone, because where something has gone wrong there is always broken relationship. We were created to live in perfect relationship with God and with one another and with all creation, and where there's brokenness, where it ripples out, where discipline has to be exercised, I can't create an outcome that makes everyone happy. I care for the people involved, though they often won't see that at the time. Often they will be angry, and while I have to recall that I am flawed, human Rachel, I also have to say, but I am your bishop, and this is my task. So, I will live this authority and I will say those hard things. I can't pretend that it's easy.

Some of the discomfort we have with people occupying positions of authority has a lot to do with blame, and a lot to do with envy. When we think everyone else is doing a better job than us, we can get envious; when we think we could do a better job than someone else, we can blame them. For example, in the church there is the situation in which people sitting in a pew can view the power as being with the PCC and might want to blame them; and the PCC might see power as being with a deanery, diocesan or general synod and might blame them; yet the synods see the bishops as the ones holding the power and choose to blame them. And we can go full circle, because we believe the myth that power is ultimately located in one place. But we all need to recognize the power and responsibility we each have, instead of staying with blame and envy, which are both about feeling powerless. I have a voice not to speak out for the voiceless, but to lift up those who feel they are voiceless, to allow them to realize their power.

I think about the word power often. As a speech and language therapist, I learnt that language shapes culture. When we use words like power, support, authority, we rarely take time to define exactly what we mean. We could be having a conversation about power and talking about completely different things. When someone tells me I have power, I want to say, 'That's right, I do. But what do you mean by that?' Power can be a positive word and it can be a dirty word. Power is about how you influence people and the world around you. Bad power is when people are trying to dominate others, lord it over them, manipulate them. It comes back to people allowing themselves to feel that they're more important than other people.

That's one of the places where the church has gone dangerously wrong in the whole area of abuse. Bishops have often been treated with deference. I want people to respect me as their bishop, but I don't want people to be unquestioningly deferential. I think it was Rowan Williams who once warned a new bishop that he would be blamed for things he did not say or do, but equally he would be put on a pedestal for things he did not say or do. It's important to be honest about our failings and weaknesses. When I'm on my own in silence before God, can I look at my heart and say, 'What was my motivation for that?' Sometimes I have to admit that it was pride. At other times I need to recognize that I got it wrong, but that my motivations were right. It would be so easy not to speak out on some things which are going to get you flak, not least on social media, but sometimes my conscience tells me that I have to speak up. When I get the chance to speak in the House of Lords, I can use that surreal opportunity to speak out boldly. That feels like good power. Good power and bad power begin in our hearts. I ask myself, all the time, 'Am I genuinely trying to use this authority that's been given to me for the well-being of the kingdom of God?' Knowing, again, that I won't always get it right.

Esther is a very significant book for me, one of my favourite books in the Bible. As a child I don't think I realized it was in the Bible, but I loved it as a story. Esther was tempted to shirk her responsibility out of fear. But Mordecai says to her, 'Perhaps you've been called to the palace for such a time as this.' Perhaps we've all been called to our roles for such a time as this. So take the risk, dare to say it, dare to get it right. And know that sometimes you will get it wrong. But use your power, use your authority, use it well.

When I became a bishop, I thought that I could speak out on lots of things in the public square, but trying to speak on everything means that your words become diluted and ineffective. There are a few key areas which I speak out on, including vulnerable women and children and young people. There are also issues which come up which it's hard to speak out on. Silence can have its own voice – sometimes it's powerful in a good way, but then there are times when I was silent and could feel my palms getting clammy and I knew I had to speak.

I've done three events in the House of Lords about women in prison and women who are homeless after leaving prison. It was important to me to have someone with lived experience at each event. I've had to work out how to do that in a way that recognizes our essential equality and doesn't sensationalize a person's experience. When we want to create change, we have to ask who is missing from the table. Women who've been in prison are not a generic group, they're individuals with distinct voices. The question is how we create spaces where everyone has a voice. I don't have lots of answers to that, but I thought about it a lot when I did a placement in South Africa in 1994, leading up to the first democratic elections. My supervisor, Mark, had a big influence on me. Mark was white, and in the early days of my placement some of the men from the local township who respected Mark hugely came and said, 'The municipality are planting trees on all the streets in the town, but they haven't planted any in the township, please help us.' Mark heard them and challenged them saying, 'So what are you going to do about it?' I thought, 'Oh, that's really harsh.' But by saying that, he enabled those men to recognize their own worth and power and to go to the municipality. He literally stood behind them, but they were the ones who went and demanded trees in the township. And it happened.

That stayed with me. It made me ask, 'How do I create space to stand behind people?' And also, if I ask to hear someone's voice on an issue that affects them, am I willing to be challenged? Sometimes that feels really uncomfortable. But that's how we create spaces where people's voices can be heard. I was very conscious of becoming a bishop as a woman and that has undoubtedly affected how I use my voice. I was very aware of those before me who had spoken out to enable women to be ordained as deacons, priests and bishops. Now I endeavour to be mindful of women who haven't had the privilege that I've had, for example vulnerable women, imprisoned women. How do I stand alongside them and with them?

One of the things I've struggled with, throughout the time I've been ordained, is thinking that I've been asked to do things just because I'm a woman. I became the first woman on the senior staff team in the Diocese of London when I was asked to be an archdeacon. I'd never led a big church, and the Church of England can be obsessed with big churches and numbers. My immediate thought was to refuse the appointment, but then I reflected on the passage where Samuel is called to anoint the next king of Israel and go to the house of Jesse. It's the Cinderella of the Old Testament. All the brothers come out, and Samuel thinks, 'He's the one! Handsome, tall, good looking.' And God says to Samuel, 'God looks on the heart.' And it turns out to be David, the shepherd boy – the Cinderella. Let's acknowledge that sometimes I have been asked to do things because I'm a woman and that's okay. I've often said that to Black clergy as well. 'I am asking you to do this. You have all the gifts and skills, and yes, there are other people that could do it as well, but I'm asking you to do this because I want people to see and live diversity.' I know that there are people better qualified than me. There are probably people who could be Bishop of Gloucester far better than me. But I've been called for such a time as this.

People might expect me to feel bruised by the journey of being a female feeling called to leadership in the Church of England, but I don't think I've been alienated by the whole church per se. In fact, in many ways I've felt a great wave of support. Over the years I probably felt more alienated as a single woman. I was at an evangelical theological college, Wycliffe Hall, when the debate about women becoming priests was going on. There was a strong theology that a woman's place was to be married and to have children, which made me feel really alienated at times. For-tunately, I had a strong confidence in who I was in Christ and really believed that God had called me – I'm really grateful for that, because at times I thought I wasn't what the church wanted me to be. As it happens, I am now very happily married, and that's been a real gift. But I do worry that single people have sometimes been alienated by the church and not seen as 'enough'.

A lot of people have been bruised by the church because they haven't been accepted as who they are. They've been told what they should look like and who they should be. Or they've tried to express who they are, and their story hasn't been heard. That really erodes trust. But I want to come back to something about blame. I am being a bit controversial, but I would want to say when people have been hurt or alienated by the church, people need to name that and acknowledge it but not get stuck in a place where alienation can almost become your friend: that bruise, that wound, can become how you understand yourself. I think that's a very dangerous place to be. The anger is justified, and it's a good place to start from, but it has to lead somewhere. One of my roles as a bishop is to receive people's stories; not necessarily to agree with them, because there are always different and conflicting perspectives, but to receive them, and to hear them. That seems to be the starting point for rebuilding trust, the place where healing can begin. Where people have been hurt or damaged, I think my plea is: don't get stuck there. Don't let that be the end of your story. Don't equate the church hurting you with God hurting you. The church is made up of very broken human beings; we kid ourselves if we think otherwise.

14 August 2020

5

Stanley Hauerwas

WITH SAMUEL WELLS, JUSTIN COLEMAN AND DEBRA DEAN MURPHY

Redescription

Stanley: I can't think of any time when I thought, I've changed the conversation. Though I can think of times when I wanted to change the conversation. I've spent a good deal of time trying to do that. I was once introduced at Southwestern University in Georgetown, Texas, my undergraduate school, where I was receiving the Alumni/ae of the Year Award. It doesn't get bigger than that. I was introduced as someone who feels like water coming out of a firehose. And I thought, goodness gracious, I guess they think that at Southwestern. That may be true more widely. So that was one place, I guess, that I thought I was making a difference.

I think reframing is something that Sam and I both do rather well. And reframing is made possible by having a different narrative from the one that shaped the question. So vocabulary makes all the difference in terms of how it is embodied in the narratives that make you say the unsayable.

Sam: I've certainly sat next to Stanley when he's reframed things. And it's got me into trouble. I particularly remember (Stanley might have forgotten) we were both asked to speak to, I think it was called, the National Association of College Chaplains, or something like that. I gave what I hoped was a fairly nuanced account of the distinctiveness of Christianity in relation to other faiths, yet with a receptivity to new understandings. And Stanley said (I'm taking the expletives out), 'What Sam's been trying to tell you is that you guys are all moribund and represent a church that's passing and should never have been.' So that was a reframing. But overaccepting was the major motif of my book *Improvisation* and overaccepting is all about reframing in the light of a larger narrative. I guess I've developed ideas of reframing from Stanley. I've certainly found the way Stanley's done it immensely valuable.

One of the first times that I remember really picking it up from him was reading an essay in his neglected 1994 book, *Dispatches from the Front*, about gays in the military. It's called 'Why Gays as a Group are Morally Superior to Christians as a Group'. There was a lot of debate in the early 1990s, at the beginning of the Clinton era, about gay people in the military. It seems a very dated debate now. And Stanley has this little essay in which he talks about what terrible things gay people might do in the shower. Like they might baptize you. I still remember that being a very satisfying reframing of an absolute classic Stanley kind.

The simplest way to explain how Stanley has reshaped the conversation is that when I first studied theology in the late 1980s, there were two kinds of Christian ethics. There was deontological ethics, which is about right and wrong, and there was consequential ethics, which is about evaluating outcomes, choosing the best outcome, and finding a theory that would validate choosing the best outcome. Now there are three: virtue ethics is the third one. Virtue ethics wasn't created by Stanley. It was created by Aristotle. And Stanley wasn't the first person to revive it in the present tense. Elizabeth Anscombe is credited with that in the 1950s. Alastair MacIntyre would be a key figure in his 1981 book *After Virtue* as well, but Stanley is the pivotal figure in making of that tradition a whole Christian revival. That is Stanley's single biggest legacy, if you want to use that word. But he's done that in a way that's not become benign, because he has this emphasis on non-violence particularly, and on specific Christian practices, notably the Eucharist, which we've written about together at some length. The problem with what's happened to virtue ethics in the philosophical field is it's become a bit like *Animal Farm* – it's become indistinguishable. The animals become indistinguishable from the humans. It's blended into deontological and especially consequential ethics so much that it hardly constitutes a distinctive field any more. Whereas that's not the case in Christian ethics, largely due to Stanley's influence.

And you've got to reckon with the phenomenal number of Stanley's graduate students, probably 80 or so, of whom more than half have gone on to hold distinguished roles of their own in the academy and have made contributions in their own right. That's a lot of people; but it's still a minority report. The interesting thing that's happened is that when Stanley came in, he was the insurgent person in relation to Reinhold Niebuhr and people influenced by him. Whereas now, Stanley is still the insurgent figure, but in relation to a different crowd. Now, what I have termed subversive ethics, that's to say, ethics that's very much rooted in people's experience – gender, race and class – has so overwhelmed the field, that those who are still finding true liberation in an authentic and orthodox Christian theology are again in the minority, but they're in a different minority, as against a different majority. So what Stanley had achieved by the early 1990s was not consensus among his peers, or throughout Christian ethics by any means, but the right to a footnote in every essay, or a last chapter in almost any compendium – Stanley would be referenced as the other – 'I suppose we probably ought to think about him.' That was the very least standard that Stanley had achieved by 30 years ago. And by now people like me, I suppose, and a lot of his graduate students – well, there's a lot of us. So, it's a voice, but it's not the majority voice, for example, within the Society of Christian Ethics in America.

Stanley: The only thing that I would add to that is a commitment to trying to keep theological language in play, and how we think about the nature of Christian life. Christology is at the centre of everything I tried to do. I think my book *The Work of Theology* has not been taken into account for understanding what I have tried to do.

The Christological emphasis wasn't there from the beginning. I became self-conscious about it when I wrote *A Community of Character*, which has my essay 'Jesus and the Story of the Kingdom' in it. I began to think about the life of Jesus under the influence not only of John Howard Yoder, but of Karl Barth. Barth was so important for me early on, but I had to revisit his work when I taught a course in Christology at the University of Notre Dame. I taught the course for the Roman Catholic seminarians. I got Wolfhart Pannenberg and Walter Kasper in it. So I did a lot of homework in Christology that I don't necessarily show.

I've also written much about the church. God hasn't given up on the church yet. My hope lies in the very fact that the church exists, even in its unfaithfulness. We have faith that God will even use our unfaithfulness to witness to the giftedness of our lives, that we are creatures of a good Creator. That makes life so damned interesting.

When people ask what I want for my grandchildren, in terms of their relationship with the church, I say I hope that they be interesting Christians, and that they never get over the oddness of being Christian. Part of that oddness is having to explain a grandfather and a grandmother who would spend their lives primarily determined by this strange group of people called Christian.

Sam: I talk about four kinds of being with: being with God, with oneself, with one another and with the creation. Different people among us feel close to God in different ways. Some alone, some of us require other people, others are very much close to God when we're at home in creation. Whatever kinds of people my children come to be, if there's such a thing as a fully fledged adult (I'm not sure I'm a fully fledged adult), but later in life, in maturity (maturity is another word that Stanley would probably say isn't a theological concept), that they would feel that depth of relationship. The church actually encompasses all three of those. It's not just the second one with the other people. The church is a many-splendoured thing, and if they feel unsettled, angry, alienated or disillusioned, then, rather than walk away – and hopefully the fact that their parents have been such insiders helps – they see it's their church and it's their job to renew the church rather than somebody else's and they can take their ball away: that they take that disillusionment, that anger, that hurt, and take it as an invitation. Because Martin Luther could have said, 'Well, this church presents me with the judgement of God, and I can't find grace. So I'm going to go off and keep the cows.' But he didn't. He stayed and said the church has got to change. And whatever you think about the splits in the church, which are obviously a source of lament, you have to applaud his determination not to leave it alone.

Stanley: One of the great challenges in terms of seminary education for the formation of people in ministry is, how do you train someone to be a human being? Often people in seminary take themselves so damn seriously. And are so judgemental about other people. You want to say often to those going into the ministry, 'Just grow up. Be a human being.' To be a Christian is to be in training to be a human being, which means you can reflect on wisdom that has taken centuries to discover.

Sam and I have been engaged in an ongoing conversation, which has developed into a friendship, for 30 years. What I've learned about friendship through this particular friendship is that you can't make your friend the way you would like them. And you can't use emotional blackmail. So you therefore must be willing to let the friendship develop in ways that you hadn't anticipated. I hadn't anticipated how important it is that we stay in touch. We both work at that. Sam does me differently. When we had the conversation that Maureen Knudsen Langdoc turned into the book *In Conversation: Samuel Wells and Stanley Hauerwas*, it just seemed like we picked up the conversations we've been having for years.

Sam: If I do Stanley differently, it's perhaps because I have a different location from most of the people who I would humbly say usually misread Stanley. There are things that I spotted in Stanley fairly early on that usually don't get spotted. To give an example: early in his career, Stanley wrote a lot about why ethics wasn't fundamentally about moments of decision, but was about the formation of character way before any decision. The struggle in United Methodism is about the different elements in John Wesley, between the discipline side of Wesley, about practices and character and the Eucharist and so on, as against the more emotional, revivalist side of Wesley, which is all about conversion. The majority of Methodism in America has gone in that second direction. I don't think anyone had pointed out before I did (I don't say this as an immodest thing, just to say how somehow our friendship got on the inside of things) that this is the same distinction about decisions: the people who emphasize conversion are all about the moment of decision, whereas the discipline people are all about the development of character. So I was able to make some connections perhaps because I didn't have any skin in the game. There was nothing for me to win or lose. I was just listening to what made Stanley angry. I think a lot of the growth in our relationship was to realize Stanley was angry, but he wasn't angry with me. And then to identify why Stanley was angry. To identify that, you have to get to know somebody really well, because Stanley really is angry. It took me quite some time. In fact, I wrote a dissertation about Stanley, in which I didn't refer to the anger. Then when I turned it into a book, I added a first chapter, which isn't called (but probably could be called if it wasn't an academic book) 'Why is he so angry?' Between writing the dissertation and writing the book I had come to know him much better.

You start a friendship by telling each other what you know, and telling stories of 'When I was an undergraduate a funny thing happened', and sometimes funny stories. That's the anecdotal approach to making a relationship. You share. We came from very different backgrounds, so we had a pretty small amount of overlap. We were feeding in quite a lot of new information at that stage of our relationship. By the time we came to know each other really well, when I moved to North Carolina in 2005, we graduated, if you like, from 'This is what I know' to 'This is what I don't know and I don't think you know – shall we discover together?' That's a different level of friendship, which I've had in very few relationships in my life. This has been obviously a very precious one.

I'll be perfectly honest and say I've had people I've looked up to before whom I felt let down by. So I wasn't looking for Stanley to be my role model in any sense, or mentor. But as we said at the beginning, making these moves to reframe things was something I developed some facility in – and Stanley was the best in the business. And to do that Christologically was as good as it gets. So that drew me into Stanley. And obviously I love reading his writing. Although, I was pleased I didn't have to read the first draft sometimes. So for a person who has shaped your thinking that much to say, 'I don't know about this, what do you think?' – that's quite a threshold to go through. When we used to go to the gym together, which we did a couple of times a week, I would say, 'This is what I'm wrestling with, and I don't know what to do about it.' We would share those different things, including some things we had in common because we were both professors at the Divinity School. And some things we did differently. That was a new level. And we've never stopped being at that level. Our conversation is mostly about things we don't know how to think about, and bringing each other's insight to them. And that's a very special kind of relationship, which requires trust, knowledge, understanding, patient listening: all the best things in life, really.

As to what we'd like to reframe next, I would say I don't know who Stanley is, if he's not at work. I don't know who he is, if he's not a theologian. Stanley's just starting to come to terms with the fact that he needs to discover who he is when he's not working every moment of the day and who he is when he's not a theologian. I don't think I'm as frightened of it as he is.

Stanley: I think that's right. I have been working, just to give myself something to work on, on what I call my biography of my books. I call it 'Remembrance, Retractions and Revisions'. I am trying to remember what I think by giving a history of what I have written. I'm not planning to publish it. It's just work that gives me something to do. One of the fundamental things that Christianity does for you is it gives you something to do. Your life isn't purposeless. You've got something to do. I can't imagine not having something to do. I think in terms of answering that question for Sam: he has to learn to befriend me as I move closer to death, and I'm not going to be there. And that takes some getting used to.

Sam: I've had to think about what it will feel like when Stanley dies. What I want to do is not do what I've done with other significant losses. What I've done with other significant losses is to create emotional space between me and the other person so that losing them won't hurt me too much. I don't think I'm the only person that's done that in the history of the world. But it can do a lot of damage to the relationship. And I don't think it really ever succeeds. You can't affect who you dream about, you can't affect who upsets you. You can't affect those things by disciplining yourself. So I think it's best not to even try. I made that mistake at a formative stage in my younger years, and I don't want to make that mistake with Stanley. The difference, of course, is we have physical distance now. We're 3,500 miles apart. The news is that during Covid Stanley has discovered Zoom, which is one of the silver linings of the pandemic. I'm sorry the rest of the world had to suffer in order for that to be so. So we can be close in all the ways in which Zoom isn't real presence but is a whole lot better than absence. But I'm a grown-up now. So the way I think isn't probably going to change a whole lot in the last third of my life. Something's left an indelible mark. The difference between now and

20 years ago is that 20 years ago I would say, 'I wonder what Stanley thinks.' Now, more often than not, I can guess what Stanley would think. So that conversation won't stop even after Stanley dies. Because I will still be thinking as we think about our parents or we think about influential people in our lives; we still think, I wonder what my mother would have thought, or I'm so sorry my mother couldn't see this day or this grandchild or whatever it might be. And I understand there will undoubtedly be a person like that for me. It could be ten years after Stanley's death, and I would still be thinking, expletives deleted, what a load of rubbish this new theological idea is, or he would have a one-liner that would completely nail something that had happened or a fight that had taken place. And I would probably be able to come close to articulating that myself, because I know Stanley so well. But I still would probably break down in tears, because I couldn't hear him say it.

Stanley: I've written about death, but I now think I needed to think more about the process of growing old. I really don't like it. I don't have a constructive response to growing old. I turned 80 this summer. You have a sense that 80 is old by reading the obituaries which report that someone died at 71. That gets your attention. My way of dealing with it is to cut the yard. I have a push mower – it's not a ride mower. When you're a theologian you never seem to finish anything. You write something and you think it was pretty good, but later you think that is not quite right. But when you cut the yard, you can look at it afterwards, and you can think that looks pretty good. I'm going to miss being able to cut the yard. I'm not going to be able to do it much longer. So physical things get you down. And I'm not as quick mentally. The implications of growing old is something most of us hadn't thought about in terms of our lives.

Sam: As to how friendship is preparation for dying, as I see it the whole universe was created so God could be with us in Christ. That's the purpose of everything we discover. We get inklings into what that relationship can be like in our friendships with one another. For one thing, it takes the sentimentality out of God's relationship with the world in Christ. Because you get cross with each other, and you forget things, and it's just very human. So the question that lurks over all our lives is, will that quality of *being with* be erased at death? In other words, will the God who has gone to such lengths to be with us in Christ still be with us on the other side of death? To be a Christian is to believe that, as that was true of Christ, that will be true of us. So, friendship gives us an insight into the joy, both the heavenly joy and the earthly durability, of what being with one another might mean. To me, friendship is as good as it gets in our imperfect existence.

Stanley: I have a name that I would put to that: Stuart Henry. Sam never knew Stuart. Stuart taught American church history at Duke Divinity School. He was a southern gentleman bachelor. He was classically the gentleman that the South allegedly produced. He was a Presbyterian minister, who was condemned to live around Methodists. He was a person who had never said 'damn' in his life. He directed many dissertations. One thing people could not understand was how Stuart and I were very good friends. We met and visited almost every morning when he came in. He always drove a grey Buick and he wore grey suits. He gave me the gift of letting me watch him grow old and die. Because when you grow old, if your weaknesses are exposed, somebody may try to help you. And that help can be a real burden. But Stuart let me be with him as he slowly lost his power to negotiate his life. And that's a great gift. Because you must learn to be with someone in their decline.

I've never been kind to myself. I work, and if you were raised a bricklayer, there's no kindness. My father was extraordinarily kind, but the work wasn't.

Sam: I am privileged to be allowed to love Stanley because there's the bark there, and you have to not take that personally. It's not directed at you. It's directed at himself. Like a lot of people, Stanley is much harder on himself than he is on others. I think I am gentler with myself than Stanley is with himself. I certainly know that routine is important. I found lockdown a lot easier than the easing of lockdown because in lockdown it was very simple. There were rules. They weren't nice rules, but you knew what they were. But the easing of lockdown has made routine harder to find, because establishing a good routine has been really hard; there's this tremendous sense of unsettledness. I have been kind to myself after some of our ghastly redundancy consultations. Not ghastly because the staff are ghastly, just ghastly because it's so painful to have to walk with people and say to them, we don't have a job for you – when they've done nothing wrong. I've been kind to myself by allowing myself the next hour to write a bit of a book that I've been working on, because that's my best way to decompress. And not to cry, basically. So, to put my energies into something constructive – that's been being kind to myself. There's probably been a higher percentage of chocolate consumed in the last six months than would probably be widely acknowledged outside the privacy of this conversation. We all need a bit of cheering up. More seriously, I've tried to put in place checking in with people for their good and for mine, which sometimes means taking a bit of time out of the working day. There are some problems in life that just throwing more time and work at don't resolve. Sometimes distance and somebody else's perspective are a better approach.

Stanley: I don't think I'm particularly kind to myself, but I live a wonderful life. I am happily married. I have a wonderful home to live in. I have a wonderful church to go to. How would you think that you haven't been wonderfully favoured? I have had wonderful students and wonderful friends.

Sam: I think Stanley just described what it means for him to be kind to himself when he talked about this book he's been writing that's not intended for publication. (Not that I believe that for one moment.) Stanley has had a self-denying ordinance for about 25 years, which is not to cross-reference his own work. He's not the kind of person all of whose footnotes are not to Karl Barth and Thomas Aquinas, but to his other books. He's not that kind of person at all. He did do a bit of that in his early work, and he consciously stopped doing it. So his 1998 self would regard the piece of what he's doing now as self-indulgence. Now he's saying, I'm going to do this because I'd like to. Stanley has worked so hard. He's had more graduate students than any other professor at Duke University, in any field. So he's read an awful lot of first drafts of chapter 4 of a dissertation about who knows what, and got comments back to the student by the following morning. He has an astonishing ability to do that. Some of that's because he loves it, and some is an overdeveloped sense of duty. And then there's other things that Stanley's done in his life that very, very few people would do, which are probably not appropriate to talk about here, but that he's done out of an overdeveloped sense of determination and duty, which a lot of people wouldn't share. So I'm encouraged to hear that he's writing a book for him. That seems to be very healthy self-care. That's a phrase that, of course, Stanley would despise.

Stanley: Exactly. I think *Vision and Virtue* (1974), maybe *Truthfulness and Tragedy* (1977), were the last time I did any cross-referencing. I had the view that if you don't cross-reference it will invite people like Sam to figure out what the connections may be. I don't want that to be made redundant, by me doing the cross-referencing. It should be work to read me. Just like it's work to read Barth.

Sam: As to what's saving my life right now – a question Barbara Brown Taylor likes to ask – the first thing that comes to my mind is that I preached a sermon on Easter Day. And I was approached by a publisher to say, 'Could you turn that into a book?' It's a book of apologetics – that's to say, a book responding to all the criticisms that are made of Christian faith. I'm really, really enjoying writing it. In fact, that was the book that I wrote two paragraphs of after the redundancy call I just referred to five minutes ago. The reason it's saving my life is because the pandemic is throwing up on a personal and public level a great number of reasons for not being a Christian – reasons why being a Christian is difficult or challenging. There may be people who think if you've written books and been a public figure in a way that Stanley has, and to a lesser extent I have, you don't get these feelings. But you do. So this opportunity gave me permission to sit down with what I identified as the ten great criticisms of Christianity, and dig deeply into what I really believe about all of those things, and to which of them I have to shrug my shoulders and say, 'Yeah, I haven't got an answer for you there.' And to which of them I could say, 'Well, actually, that isn't really the question you think it is. And if you turn it round and reframe it, it looks very different.' I found that on a spiritual and emotional level really rewarding. It's a place to put and resolve a lot of my exasperation about the day job, because it's been quite challenging, leading St Martin's through this very, very demanding period for everybody. So the permission, the invitation to think about that at some length and record my thoughts, has been a blessing to me.

Stanley: For me, it's reflections on what a wonderful life I've had, that has drawn so many wonderful people into my life in a way that gives me wonderfully happy memories. That gets you through a lot.

* * *

Justin: Years ago when I was an associate pastor at the church at which I'm now senior pastor (University United Methodist Church, Chapel Hill, North Carolina), I facilitated several rounds of book studies on Stanley and Sam's *Blackwell Companion to Christian Ethics*. It's not a book that I would typically use in a book study with a congregation, but our congregation was excited to tackle issues of Christian ethics within the scope of Christian liturgy. I would add that of all the studies I've done, particularly book studies, the *Blackwell Companion to Christian Ethics* study has been the most well loved. I think the study is resonant because the members of the Christian communities that I've been a part of have longed to see a vision of the church that takes the gospel seriously – that takes Jesus seriously. Some might call it a radical vision. These congregants simply believed this vision was the calling of the church – the calling of the people of God – and they were very interested in immersing themselves in a conversation where the writers seemed to be taking scripture seriously, in trying to do what Sam talks about in his work *Improvisation*, as they sought to understand how to live as Christians in the world. That's one of the ways that their work has been important to me.

Debra: For several years I worked as director of Christian formation at a large suburban mainline church in Raleigh, North Carolina. Everything about that work was informed by the sensibilities that Sam and Stanley share about the formative power of liturgy. Sunday school and Bible study do not exhaust what it means to be formed as Christians: formation is always happening. Now I teach undergraduates at a small church-related liberal arts college in Appalachia. And it's both a challenge and a gift to introduce students to a vision of the church more expansive and interesting than the church they think they've rejected – to tease out the political nature of the gospel, and to play with that word 'politics' in the imagination of college students. I use Sam's textbook when I teach Christian ethics, since ethics for them is usually about hot-button issues and how to decide moral quandaries. Instead we talk about stories, about forgiveness, about practices. These are all ways that my teaching is informed by the longstanding work of both Stanley and Sam. And again, in both of those contexts, it was and is both gift and challenge. I have to say, in that pretty affluent suburban congregation, they were game, for the most part, for a different way of imagining what Christian formation can be. And my students are game for that too, even though many of them have been wounded by the church and are suspicious of it. They're hungry for their imaginations to be enlarged.

In some ways, the challenge is a language problem. It's a challenge to speak a different language in a congregational setting about what it means to form disciples, when our imaginations are so schooled in the imagery and language of school and education. And with college students, it's the challenge of reorienting their thinking about what the church even is, what discipleship is, what ethics is. So the challenge is ongoing, and can be daunting. But one way to think about the gift is that when we do have those breakthroughs, when a group of older adults in a congregation or a group of first-year college students finds that they have not been formed well in the gospel, it's liberating and exciting to them. So it's a challenge and a gift at the same time, always.

Justin: I'm serving a church that is surrounded on three sides by the University of North Carolina. Our context is not dissimilar to what Debra's just described relating to her students. There is a similar sense in which, particularly among our younger demographic, people want to be challenged. People come to our church because they believe there's something about their lives that might just need to be reordered and reoriented by Jesus. Therefore, people come to church hopeful that they might be challenged. People also resist the challenges when they're offered, but, thankfully, they continue to come back and engage because they receive the conversation we are having as a gift. I absolutely resonate with everything that Debra just said.

As for tensions between Stanley and Sam's work, I have always thought of Sam as the radio edit of Stan. This has nothing necessarily to do with the explicit nature of their speech. Sam is a preacher. In my experience, as congregants have read Sam's works with me, they hear him differently because he is a preacher used to addressing people like them. Whereas Stanley's work sometimes takes a little interpretation for them.

Debra: Ever since I moved back to Appalachia (I'm actually from here, but was in North Carolina for a long time), the significance of place has emerged for me as a central way to think about theology as lived disciple-ship. I'm teaching environmental theology this fall, and we're using some of Ched Myers' work around watershed discipleship. So this isn't really so much about anything I detect in the writing of Sam and Stanley. But Sam's context is mostly secular Britain, whereas Stanley's context for a very long time has been the 'Christ-haunted' American South. So what I've often wondered, especially in the work you've done together, is not so much about tensions between those two places, but rhetorically how you try to write for an audience from your very distinct kinds of places.

Stanley: I never do typology. That's partly because as someone that went to Yale in the era of H. Richard Niebuhr's *Christ and Culture*, the game was always the person with the most inclusive typology at the end wins. Typologies are oftentimes arguments that are hidden, and I want to get those arguments out. But the main reason that I don't do typologies is I'm no good at it. I think the emphasis on narrative is an attempt to defeat generalizations that often take the form of typologies.

Sam: As to audience, I've never wanted to choose in my life between the academy and the church. And I've never wanted to choose in my writing either. Even though I've written in recent years more obviously for church and society than for the academy, I always want to write in a way that would stack up in the academy. I'd like to feel the arguments still carry weight. The great thing about when you're writing with Stanley is that in the academy, as anyone who's spent any time in the academy will know, the competition is to show who's read the most. If you're writing with Stanley, you know you're always going to win that argument. Stanley's always read more than anybody. My critics might say I don't really read, I just write – which I'd like to feel is a bit harsh. But I certainly don't read as much as Stanley does. I've piggybacked on Stanley a little bit, I hope not in bad ways, but in ways that have given me more confidence to speak more explicitly and more boldly than a lot of people (and I'm talking about friends of mine, and people I've worked alongside in academic ways, when I did my PhD, when I was a professor, and those kind of things) who feel inhibited by their awareness that they have to qualify every remark and they're terrified that someone's going to publish a book two weeks before they publish theirs, which is going to steal all their clothes. I've had fewer of those kinds of inhibitions, and that's partly because I've got a lot of that confidence from the fact Stanley has probably read it. The conversations we've had, I've often checked out and said, 'Did I miss something here?' Sometimes I did miss something, and I have to go back and do a bit more work.

But as far as place is concerned, Debra's absolutely right. We are in very different places. When I went to North Carolina, I tried to adopt an air of appreciative enquiry: I was trying to talk Duke University and North Carolina back to themselves. I was trying, almost self-consciously, to say, 'I don't know anything about this, but from what I've heard, it seems to me ...' That can be quite an interesting and useful role to play. What might be lost on my American friends is that, when I moved to London, I was doing the same. I'd never lived in London for more than a short while. I didn't really know London. I'm not a Londoner. Now I've been there several years, so I can't say that any more. But I was doing the same kind of thing. What Stanley's been doing is to do that with the church. He said, 'Well, it says here, that the Christ is the centre of all things. And it says here that following Christ means taking up your cross and following him. So why don't we go with that for a while, and see how far it takes us, in an almost innocent way.' We've got that in common. Maybe I've learned a bit of that from Stanley, that 'Tell me if I'm wrong, but I thought this was supposed to be about Jesus. I thought we were supposed to trust. I thought providence had something to do with it. I thought the Holy Spirit was supposed to be moving in this place. Nobody's telling me I'm wrong here. So why don't we go a bit further with that?' That's something I think I've learned from Stanley.

Stanley: One of the distinctions that I don't like is the distinction between theoretical and popular literature and writing. I've tried to defy that distinction. One of my favourite mystery writers is an Englishman who went to Australia named Arthur Upfield. His detective Boney Bonaparte is a half-Aboriginal, half-white person who solves mysteries using the Aboriginal way and modern techniques. One of the murder mysteries turns on the distinction between the popular and the theoretical. It's a wonderful mystery which I have deep sympathies for because it has to do with audience. If you take the essays in my first collection, *Vision and Virtue* (1974), there's one called 'Situation Ethics, Moral Notions, and

Moral Theology', which is a hard theoretical discussion that calls into question that odd distinction. In that same book, there's an essay called 'Love is Not All You Need', which is what people would call popular. But it's very serious. If you take one of my most famous chapters, namely, the chapter on *Watership Down* in *A Community of Character* (1981), can rabbits be serious? Yet I think the implications for political theory in *Watership Down* are really quite extraordinary.

Debra: Turning to where I'd like to push Sam and Stanley a little bit further: I mentioned earlier that I'm teaching environmental theology. Climate collapse is central to our exploration, partly because 'environment' is such a problematic abstraction. And this always raises the question of hope. So it's here that I want to press Sam and Stanley. Do we need a more robust account of hope in the face of climate collapse? I remember the essay Stanley wrote in 1986 called 'A Pacifist Response to *In Defense of Creation*', where he schools the United Methodist bishops on the idea of peace, that peace is not a strategy, but peace is simply the way of Jesus, whatever is going on in the world. I think there's an analogy there with hope. I think there's a way that some of what Stanley has said about peace can find some purchase on the theological idea of hope in this real ecological crisis we're in.

But I also worry sometimes – and I feel like I'm guilty of this, too – that we can lapse into the language that our hope is in God, which it is, of course. But what does that mean? And what does it look like? Because my worry, especially in talking about this with students, is that this general kind of confession – our hope is in God – says, well, therefore, there's nothing we can do. The world is going to hell, we can't stop it, or God will stop it at some point. So those are the tensions I feel with the concept of hope in this one context. It's not a fault necessarily in the work you've already done. But I think it's a challenge for the work going forward. How do we think about hope in a really robust way in the midst of this real existential crisis?

Justin: I have people saying to me, hey, Justin, you are an African American pastor. Why are you hanging out so much with these white dudes like Sam and Stan? Being fond of white male theologians doesn't play well these days. Most folks know who know me know that I've read Stan's works and consider him a good friend. I regularly receive this question: 'Why do you hang out with this older white dude? Where is liberation in Stanley's works? How often does he refer to Black theologians and womanist theologians?' So I feel as if I must prove my theological diversity credibility each time because I've spent so much time with Sam's works and with Stanley's works. I have personally never felt that Stanley carried his white privilege in a way that was offensive to me as an African American. And as an African American theologian, I've actually felt that he and Sam have taken on issues that really come close to conversations in the Black community and conversations for people of colour. But people are looking for explicit decrying of the things that are harming people of colour and have wanted more of that. The one place that I might have felt a little bit of tension, especially in the early days, is around how politics is engaged. I've known clergy who have held public office, and some of those have pastored churches I've attended over the years. These clergy have believed and taught that to be an African American clergy person means one must engage politics head on. And not just the politics of Jesus here: finding affiliation, moving into a place where you can make an impact, and letting that be a place of resistance. I've sometimes held this kind of political action a bit lightly. I'm very concerned that in my congregation, and every congregation I've ever served, there have been people who have not been able to distinguish clearly what it means to be a Christian over against what it means to be a Democrat or a Republican. I've worried this lack of distinction could easily be the case for me as well. The ability to be critical about these things is a gift I've received because of the way I have read Stanley.

Stanley: It's tricky, because I resist singular accounts of the gospel, such as the word liberation. I, of course, care deeply about ending the kind of racism that has been part and parcel of our lives. It's helped to do that with a kind of discriminating language that will give us a way forward. You might think that the word 'liberation' will do that. But I think it is not concrete enough. One of the things that has to be said is, America is a slave country in which what was done was so wrong, there's nothing you can do to make it right. How to struggle with that knowledge in a way that doesn't ask African Americans to continue to pay the price for America's unwillingness to recognize it is a challenge I think it's been very difficult to put politically. I'm more than ready to take the leadership of African Americans to tell me what to do. But that's tricky. It's those kinds of complexities that continue to make any way I move on these questions problematic.

Justin: I tend to agree, and this agreement has got me in trouble. The danger of these single narratives, as Stan would say, is allowing all of one's theology to flow from them. I do think this can be problematic. However, when it comes to race in this cultural moment, what I have seen among African American pastors and theologians is a real pressure to end equivocation and abandon dialectics and say, 'No, there's something at stake here. We need people to stop holding contradictions in tension, and part of the way we know that you're with us is how you respond with a kind of firm anti-racist orthopraxy in the midst of this anti-Black society.' You have to be able to name racism clearly and not let people off easy with lofty forgiveness and reconciliation language. I want language of liberation and healing – I want to talk about the sin and how one can be saved and reconciled to God and humanity. I went to two seminaries. In the first seminary, I read more liberation theology, Black theology and womanist theology than Augustine for sure in those introductory classes, and so I came to Duke steeped in those conversations before I moved on to anything that one might consider more classical theology. So those theologies live in me. But I am also concerned that we have an evangelical view of liberation. We have to be able to name the sin and the restoration. I'm going back and forth here because I do think it's a bit of a dance. This is like dancing double Dutch – two jump ropes moving in opposing directions. I think learning how to do that dance and learning the balance in theology and practice is really important.

On the other hand, theology taught in a majority-white context in an unexamined way can unintentionally assume whiteness as normative. What some pastors and theologians of colour are saying is that just theology as seen from a Black or Korean perspective can be as distinctive as Black church or Korean church cultural expressions can be. The cultural perspective and social location of these voices matter for theology. I'm pastor of a predominantly white United Methodist church. I'm one of the few African Americans in our congregation. When people talk about church, they assume that their cultural experience of our church is the norm, everything else is something like take-out. I just feel in the mood for Black church today, or I feel in the mood for a Latinx church today. But the white-majority church is just an a-cultural church. White churches don't always realize that they are as much a cultural expression as any other church. I want to name that. It is the case that it's really hard to do theology in a way that honours diverse cultural perspectives. It might even be impossible for us to do theology in a way that doesn't require compound nouns – Black theology, liberation theology, womanist theology, etc. I try to be aware of this as I practise theology.

Debra: There can be a lot of white hand-wringing about the kind of issues Stanley just named, which are serious – the inadequacy of descriptors and a certain necessary language. But ultimately part of the question is: what stake do Christians have in seeing to the preservation of certain democratic institutions that support vulnerable communities? It's the messiness of politics. I do think some theology can have a sort of 'opt out' feel. That's also a function of privilege. But we're in the messy materiality of this particular moment when so much is at stake, when so many safety nets, like the Affordable Care Act, may go away with this next Supreme Court appointee.[2] Do Christians have a stake in trying to keep that from happening? This is at the forefront in the relationship between politics and church, Christianity and the social order. I'm not sure it's a time when we can opt out, even if we think we have a theological or philosophical rationale for doing so.

Sam: I'm going to do a real Stanley move. Stanley is a great one for saying I think I said something in a book that I wrote in 1982 that people haven't paid sufficient attention to. I don't think I've ever used that line before. It's such a Stanley line, I can't resist using it today. In my first book, I made a distinction between truth and truthfulness. I was attempting to talk about Stanley's work, and the point that I was making was, 'Show me the money', which is the theological move that Stanley makes that I think not enough people have noticed. And I'm genuinely not joking this time. What I picked up on is that he says: it's not true theology unless it turns into genuine community, unless it's lived out in lives. So my understanding of the liberation conversation Justin and Stanley were just having is this. In the middle of Exodus we have these two fundamental events: we have Exodus 14—15, the crossing of the Red Sea, liberation. Then we have Exodus 19—20, covenant, the Ten Commandments. Liberation and covenant have got to be held together. Liberation on its own without covenant is not freedom. But covenant without liberation is a prison. Not all of us are pastors, but Justin's and my role, as pastors, is to lead congregations towards a new covenant to embody forth the truth of liberation. That's the *semper reformanda*, it's a refiner's fire, it's got to keep getting better and better. In different generations, different issues present themselves. Clearly in the 1860s, where you stood on slavery was absolutely foundational, you couldn't get past it. What the Black Lives Matter movement has put on the agenda is: you can't say we don't talk about race here, that's politics or something. If it was ever a legitimate thing to say, it certainly isn't now. Every congregation has to show that it is a congregation in which all the children of God flourish and contribute.

The problem with racism for the church is that by excluding some voices the church is diminished and can't fully be the church. So my reluctance to speak in the public sphere about race isn't just, 'What's a white guy doing talking about this?' It's that my first job is to shape a community that can be an example to the world of the truthfulness of the

---

2 Amy Coney Barrett, a noted conservative, took her place as a Supreme Court Justice on 27 October 2020.

gospel. If I've had some success at that, you know, maybe in spite of my ministry, through my colleagues' ministry, or through the congregation, if we're making some progress, then I can say, come and see; then I can say, I think we've learned some things together I want to share. But if I'm a pastor of a congregation, and have had zero success in my home community of getting this balance between liberation and covenant, and then I go and tell the world how they should organize their affairs, I'd deserve to be laughed out of court. I'd like to feel I've kept my mouth shut when I cannot point to a good example of what I'm trying to propound. And if I can't point to a good example, in a certain instance, that would be my version of Stanley saying that's theoretical.

Justin: This comes up often when we talk about race. The proof of the pudding is in the eating, as they say. Where is the lived example? The questions that we ask on the ground about racism here are, 'How does racism manifest itself? How is racism manifested in your life and in the lives of people around you?' Everyone ought to have something to say about that. I'd also say, when I think about my own reluctance to speak about race as a pastor of a predominantly white church, I withhold something every Sunday. Why do I withhold something every Sunday? Because if I don't withhold every Sunday, I won't last here very long. Now, is that because I am not courageous and am afraid to tell the truth? This could be the case. Mostly, it's because I believe that occupying this office is a place of necessary resistance. If I don't give these relationships time, with the ability for me as an African American to sit and talk with white congregants about how we see and understand the world differently at times – if I don't allow time for that, then there will be a lost opportunity for true reconciliation. Reconciliation, I might add, is a word I don't use very often these days, because I think it has too often been used poorly. As a pastor committed to reconciliation or racial healing, I believe I've got to play a longer game. Because if every relationship with an African American church staff member is short-lived, then this church may never learn to have deeper conversations. Therefore, I believe there's a necessity to withholding. I'm thankful to have family members who will tell me if they feel I've withheld too much, and will also tell me if they think that I've not shared enough. Again, there's a dance. That's part of the double-Dutch image I used before.

Stanley: It has also to do with the complexity of our relationships. Justin and I share a Friday night football game. We're both Texans. We understand what it means to score a touchdown. That's a silly example. But it nonetheless indicates that you need to build up from all kinds of relationships, to be able to identify yourself as Christians. One of the things that is oftentimes not mentioned, as part of this, is class. I was raised as a working-class white in the same jobs that African Americans perform. That also gives you a sense of appreciation for one another. It's the kind of thing that we need to find more and more ways to learn. Eleven o'clock on Sunday morning, as Martin Luther King said, is the most segregated time in America. That's a chilling fact. If I were an African American, I wouldn't want whites taking over my church. So how do you negotiate these matters?

Justin: It works both ways. I have a congregation that if the demographics change more than 25 per cent, the congregation members who are in the 75 per cent believe that their congregation has been taken away from them. Studies show that a 25 per cent shift represents a tipping point. A congregation like mine might say, 'Hey, we have this African American pastor. We want more African Americans, but only so many.' The challenge, again, is around friendship. Unless we develop the kinds of friendships in Christ that can help us to name and talk about difficult issues such as the problem of race, then we won't move forward well as Christian people. Those of us in intentionally cross-racial spaces meant to promote racial healing must be willing to devote time to the developing of friendships that can lead to ways of truth.

Debra: My context is academic. A classroom is a community. At least that's what we try to foster. And there are intersections there – multiple sites of oppression and identity that have to be noted. And for me the question of when to speak, when not to speak, is about my role. I'm in charge of directing and facilitating conversation and learning. There's a time not to speak. There's a time for us to recognize that we can't fix this with the right reading or the right words. I am at a small liberal arts college in Appalachia, but we have students from a lot of places. We have students from Appalachia, we have international students. It's really hard sometimes not to expect our minority students, whether African American or transgender, to educate us. We have a lot more work to do ourselves in majority-culture social spaces. We should not expect to be schooled on what those sites of oppression look like. But it does, again, come down to what kind of a community we're going to be and how we're going to try to navigate that.

In terms of forming the imaginations and character for such a time as this, I begin every one of my classes with a few minutes of guided meditation. It's pretty non-confessional, actually, but we do it. And I've been in the habit for the last couple of years of using the circle process from

44

the restorative justice movement as a way to have conversations that are less about noting how many people raise their hand, and more about how to cultivate real listening. When we've put those kinds of practices in place, we have a chance, as the semester goes on, to succeed in the work that the bureaucracies think we're doing, which is training people for future remunerative employment. But from my perspective, forming these persons to be committed to the flourishing of themselves and others is the real goal. So we're quiet, we're silent. We try to listen. And we try to engage the work.

Stanley: As to experiencing joy, there's a story in Texas about religious freedom day, which we used to have in the public schools. Children were asked to bring in symbols of their faith. The Jewish child brought in and said, 'This is the menorah.' The Catholic child came in and said, 'This is the crucifix.' Then the United Methodist child came in and said, 'This is a baking dish.' The child was thinking of Wednesday night potluck dinners. It was so strong in that way. I'm going to be extremely happy when we can come back together and celebrate the Eucharist as a body. I really miss it. It reminds me how important the worship of God is for making me joyful.

Sam: One of the things I'm most proud of about my community, St Martin's, is the way it's teaching the church about how to think about disability. We've got our annual disability conference coming up online in a couple of weeks. I was asked to talk at last year's conference about neurodiversity. I'm currently reading a book about autism in the church, and I'm learning on every page. You can use a word like diversity as a slogan. But I'm learning that, beneath the slogan, if you sit down and you actually read and you listen to it, you know, the thing about that conference is that the speaking parts are almost all taken by people with lived experience. So if you go back to the hand-wringing point Debra made, it's not a bunch of theologians or pastors or Christians saying what can we do about them, it's changing who's sitting at the feet of whom. You can say as much of that as you like in theory, but to do it in practice has been important.

On a personal level, I always say friendship is the centre of my life. And there have been a very few friends I felt I was allowed to hug or they felt I was allowed to hug, not being sure if we were going to be fined hundreds of pounds for doing so. And there have been friends I simply couldn't hug, either because I couldn't see them or because we both felt that wasn't something we could do. And in that not hugging and yet loving, that rediscovering a way to relate, you have to overcompensate in other ways. As everybody knows, Stanley's a close friend of mine. Zoom can't give you some things in friendships, but it can give you other things. So I would say the fact that the lockdown and everything has disabled everybody has put me in touch with what I have to learn from people who've always had that experience. But then, secondly, the disability of the lockdown has made me improvise in how I express intimacy with those I really care about.

Debra: I echo Stanley's grief in not sharing the Eucharist in person. What has it meant to be hungry for the Eucharist since mid-March of 2020? My school is all online. I actually came to my office today, which I don't do very often. The lack of embodiment really is something to grieve. So it's taking pleasure in small joys. And I agree with Sam, that there have been some gifts in Zoom-world that I would not have anticipated. In a classroom where students are looking at the back of each other's heads, and I can't even see all of them, the democratization of space online, where everybody has equal visibility, has opened up some possibilities for connections and conversation that I know we wouldn't have had when we were in person. So there are small joys for which I'm grateful.

Justin: The generosity of our local congregation as it has sought to walk alongside those who are on the margins. Our community has been beautiful to see during this pandemic period. I would also say friends – friends that I can call or Zoom call to laugh and cry with – have been critical. There's been a joy in parenting: I have three sons ranging from 6 to 14. There have been some really tough days, particularly in virtual education, but there have also been moments of great joy. Being a parent when I'm with my kids all the time has been one of those joys. I'm like Debra, today has been one of the few times I've come to the office, just because I wanted to be able to better control the volume around me. There have been deep joys during time at home with family. I have also spent more time out with my barbecue grill and smoker, making Texas brisket, which Stanley will appreciate. And I must say it is a deep joy. I know not everyone prefers such a diet, but, oh my goodness, what joy to be able to enjoy it with those who do.

10 and 24 September 2020

6

Barbara Brown Taylor

Imagination

Sam, you began this conversation by asking me, 'Where are you?' I like that question very much, since physical location has so much to do with mental outlook. It's God's question to Adam and Eve in the Garden of Eden, after their eyes have been opened by their encounter with the serpent and they know for the first time that they are naked. I'm clothed, but where I am is my own kind of Eden – 150 acres in rural north-east Georgia with three freshwater springs, two streams, one river and a lot of creatures who keep the woods and pastures humming with life. My husband Ed and I have lived here since the early 1990s, when I came to Clarkesville, Georgia, to serve a small Episcopal church (population 1,500). It's the only Episcopal church in the whole county, which means that it is impossible to live in a silo here. If you want to go to an Episcopal church, you have one choice. You will sit next to people who cancel out your vote and people who wouldn't let their children read your books.

During the last US presidential election, I put a sign by my mailbox that was unlike any of the others in my neighbourhood. When people passed it coming in, they said, 'Aren't you afraid to put that by your mailbox?' I *was* a bit afraid, but since I've made mistakes about my neighbours based on the signs in their yards, I thought it was only fair to let them know that they might have made mistakes about me based on the sign in mine. The political imagination pushes one towards the absolutes of two mutually exclusive groups. In that version of reality, the realization of my hopes means that someone else's must be dashed, and the realization of their hopes means the same thing for me. I refuse to settle for that version of reality. I buy my eggs from a man who does not see the world the way I do. They are very good eggs. Like a lot of my neighbours, he and his wife look after the sick, mourn the dead, make casseroles for people who are behind on their rent, share their hay with people who have run out, and help tow stranded cars out of ditches. I know those things about them. What I don't know is why they lean right while I lean left. So I'm willing to give them the benefit of the doubt, and hope they'll do the same for me.

Meanwhile they help me remember that it's good to reflect on questions of social class in The Episcopal Church. A joke I have heard more than once in the US is that when Christians went west to evangelize, the Baptists went on foot, the Methodists went on horses, and the Episcopalians went in their Pullman cars. Where I live, things are a bit different from that. The Episcopal church is where the odd people go – the ones who don't fit easily into the other mainline churches. You don't have to bring your zippered Bible to worship. You can, but no one's going to vet you on your biblical interpretation, any more than they are going to ask you if you're in line with Episcopal beliefs. They're going to hand you a prayer book instead, with prayers that have come down from centuries ago, and they're going to welcome you into a fellowship of odd people. Some of them are saints; all of them are sinners. In my town, most of the eccentric people finally wander into the Episcopal church because they have tried everything else. If they stay, it's because they have finally found their crowd.

I realized I had a facility for words when I was in the first or second grade. In retrospect, it had a lot to do with my family moving a lot and being academic types. During uprooted and sometimes scary times, books opened the world to me and allowed me to imagine an alternative kind of life. It made me want to be a writer, before I knew what that way of life entailed: a lot of time standing apart from people to notice things no one else was noticing, followed by more time alone writing those things down while other people were busy living them. It's hard when you're trying to express the inexpressible or even get close to what is expressible. You try out 27 words before the twenty-eighth finally sounds a little closer to the truth. I know a lot of people who want to be writers, but not nearly as many who want to spend much time writing.

I would love to write fiction, but that's a different kind of gift. When I try to write fiction, it feels like I'm lying – just making things up. Which is the point! When I read fiction, it seems truer than true – not lies at all. But I don't have the knack for writing it. Early in my career, I managed to get a short story reviewed by an editor of *Harper's Magazine*. At the bottom of the first page, the editor wrote, 'Very good writing, but it makes me want to kill myself.' I'm better off with what I do now – essays, talks and first-person narrative.

I used to read much more than I do now. I read intentionally, but not just to keep my writing alive. I read to immerse myself in other worlds. I don't have for ever to live, so I borrow lives. Every time I read a fantastic book, I get another one. I'll never lose my family to the Holocaust. I'll never fight in a South American revolution, or escape from a Tibetan Buddhist monastery to discover how most people live. But every time

I read a book that immerses me in such experiences, I get an extra life. That's what motivates my reading life. I think of fiction as embodied theology, or embodied faith, or embodied wretchedness: there's something about the fiction that enlarges my life with others and I can't get enough of it.

I have an intentional rotation between international writers, regional writers, men, women, people of colour. I live in a tiny rural county, so if I want diversity in my work, I can either spend all of my time in front of a computer screen or I can read books. Lately I have been reading a lot of Howard Thurman's work. He wasn't a novelist, but he wrote like one. What a gift for language! He's been on my shelf since college, which means someone required me to read him in college. He was a grandfather of the American civil rights movement, but more of a mystic than an activist. He co-founded the first interracial, intercultural and interreligious church in the United States. He was the first Black dean of chapel at a predominantly white American university. *Life* magazine recognized him as one of the 12 great preachers who were bringing people back to church in 1953 – a full 11 years before the passage of the Civil Rights Act in the US. His best-known book, *Jesus and the Disinherited*, is as fresh today as it ever was. And yet his name is unknown to so many people. I hope that changes soon.

I never get bored with the Bible, largely because my Episcopal tradition has freed me from a certain way of reading scripture. I think it was Marcus Borg who said that there's a difference between reading scripture literally and literarily. The literary layers are so remarkable. I've been helped a great deal by Jewish friends who say, 'Why do you read scripture like it's a driving manual? For us, Torah is something you argue about – something you look at this way, that way and the other way around. Then you tell a story, and you ask another question.' I've come newly alive to the Bible as I read it with other people who are willing to have a sacred debate about it. It's the narrative that knocks me out. I'm sure scripture is inspired, but not in the way most people think. It's inspired in its narrative brilliance, its word-choices, its discrepancies, its humanity. I wish I could read it in its original languages. That's one of my holy envies – of Muslim friends who can read Arabic, who know their sacred text in the same tongue it was written in.

I recently received a three-page handwritten letter from a woman I don't know. She wrote to me because she had begun to read the Bible. She was shocked, she said – truly shocked – to see what was actually there. By the time she got to the end of Genesis, she had three pages of questions to ask me. She said, 'I've been teaching the teenage Sunday school class at my church. How can I go back now? Now that I know what is really in this book? And we give it to children!' She was undone. To reclaim the Bible for the broad church will require reading it – and reading a lot of it, not just the favourite chapter of the favourite Gospel or the favourite song. That's going to raise difficult questions for people who've never done that before. We have an educational project before there's a reclaiming project, but I'm not sure how many people in this country are interested in the educational project.

I came to Christianity when I was a teenager through a fundamentalist church, which meant that I had a very narrow view of the Bible – mostly the frightening stuff. But in seminary I took an Old Testament survey course from Brevard Childs, who gave me challenging assignments and put wonderful notes in the margins of my papers. He was the first person to ask me to read a text at any depth. Once I learned to do that, I asked, 'What else have I been missing?' So many Christians seem to believe that biblically based sermons are about getting everyone lined up on the main road, going in the same direction. Lately, I've been using sermons to ask questions instead. Instead of confirming the conventional reading of a passage, I ask things like, 'Why do you suppose we read it that way?' Or, 'What else might it mean?' Take the Beatitudes, for instance – especially Luke's version of them, in which Jesus not only says, 'Blessed are you who are poor', but also, 'Woe to you who are rich.' The meaning of that passage has a lot to do with which one you are – poor or rich? There are two different sermons there at least.

Theological imagination is imagination about life. At least half of Jesus' project in his lifetime was leading people to reimagine the neighbour, the self, the world and the divine. Was God a distant monarch or a parent? Was the neighbour someone a lot like you who lived next door, or was the neighbour anyone in need of your mercy? Did the world belong to the Lord God or to the Lord Caesar? I'm convinced Jesus was engaged in the struggle to free people from the imperial imagination. The more I've studied the New Testament and the ways in which Jesus used language to reach people, shock them, anger and inspire them, the more I've tried to follow him in that way. How can I use language to shift my listener's view of reality – even the tiniest degree? Because if I can find the right words to do that, a shift will take place in the listener as well. To see the world differently is to entertain the possibility of living in it differently. This imaginative task has been especially vital during the pandemic, when we haven't been able to share bread, wine, water or breath. Our imaginations have been working overtime during this period of fasting from those things.

When I speak of the theological imagination, I'm not thinking of anything as sophisticated as Christology or ontology. I'm just thinking about how we see the world and God's place in it, which includes everything from politics to economics to climate change to religion. It's easy to forget that most of the New Testament was written after the destruction of Jerusalem in 70 CE, which means it was written while Jesus' Jewish followers were trying to imagine their lives after that disaster. What a task! People who talk about imagination as if it's making things up are overlooking one of the most powerful faculties that human beings have. But powerful things can go both ways. At the moment the human imagination seems overheated with enemy-thinking, self-defence and scenarios of doom. That's why I like to read the local newspaper and go for long walks around my small town – to keep grounding my imagination in the real world where I live, as a way of surviving the headlines.

I have a friend who's a pastor of a big church in New York City. He gathered his staff recently and asked, 'What do we want to preserve from the pandemic? What have we gained during this time that we don't want to let go?' That question shifted my perspective. It reminded me that good and bad don't come in separate packages. Life and death are always intertwined. Since I live on a farm, I spend a lot of time with dirt: manure, compost, leaf rot, garden soil. During the pandemic I have had my hands in it more than ever before – digging things up, burying things, planting things – and of course thinking about how I too will be buried one day, which may be sooner than later. So that's what I want to preserve from the pandemic – this sobering, life-giving practice of playing in the dirt. As it says in Genesis, 'Dust thou art, and to dust shalt thou return.' In light of that, making friends with the dirt – the dust – seems like a profoundly faithful thing to do.

8 October 2020

7

Kelly Brown Douglas
Justice

There's justice and then there's social justice. When we talk about justice, it's easy to talk in the abstract. Who's going to say they don't support justice? But it's one thing to make a commitment to justice in the abstract, and it's quite another thing to begin to enact that. What does justice look like? How does it play out? We can *talk* about justice, but the only way we *know* justice is if it becomes incarnate – if it is lived out in history. That's what social justice does for us. It grounds our so-called commitment to justice and makes the abstract real in the ways we live together. The social part of justice is the way we relate one to another as interesting, complicated communities. Our tradition has the incarnation at the centre, so everything we commit to must be manifest and embodied in history.

We're all in this struggle together – to move toward a more just society. What's the peculiarity of the manifestation of this in America? We can talk about this on a couple of levels. First, what's interesting about our so-called democracy and its founding is that America is made of two warring souls, right from its inception. On the one hand, this is a nation founded on the notion of Anglo-Saxon exceptionalism. America was going to be the city on the hill, carrying forth this notion that Anglo-Saxons had a unique sense of moral values, a unique sense of how to create justice and democracy. That was translated into our context as American exceptionalism. That's always defined America, especially in terms of race – America is always raced white. Which is how white supremacy came to be in the very foundation, the very DNA of this country.

Yet America was also able to give birth to a vision of being a true democracy, where there was freedom and justice for all, where everyone has inalienable, God-given rights to life, liberty and the pursuit of happiness. It was always a limited vision of democracy, but it gave voice to a vision of our better angels. From the very inception of America, these two things have always been in conflict – and that conflict has always been a raced conflict. Furthermore, there's always been a narrative of anti-Blackness that runs beneath Anglo-Saxon white supremacist exceptionalism. It continues to play itself out in our history. There are certain times when it becomes most visible, but it's always there. Those are the competing forces.

In a nation that considers itself a beacon, with all its imperialist motives, we're going to get these conflicts. Capitalist systems of power thrive through inequality – not everybody is going to get an equal piece of the pie, which is their due in respect of their humanity. When you have a capitalist structure joined with a nation that is grounded in the kind of raced narratives that our nation is grounded in, the result is systemic racial oppression. I always say that to call ourselves a democracy is aspirational: it's something that we must continue to live into. But we have a competing narrative that impedes us from doing that. That's America. It's not unique to who we are, because we know that poverty and white supremacy are global issues, and that they have their own specific, local manifestations. But we have to reckon with the fact that, despite our founding myth, not all people are treated as if they are really created equal.

The phrase 'Black bodies' becomes very significant here. From the moment that Black people, African people, were stripped from their land, captured and enslaved, they were no longer seen as human beings, and were instead seen as labouring bodies, as objects. This country gave birth to chattel slavery – not slavery, but chattel slavery, which is a different thing altogether, because chattel slavery separated a people from their humanity and labelled them as property. When you think of bodies as property, you don't think of them as vulnerable, real human beings. You can do anything you want with a person if you don't have to think of them as having a feeling, sensitive, human body. Black bodies have been assaulted, attacked and disregarded, as if the body isn't a person; as if the body is disembodied, disconnected from personhood. On so many levels, white supremacy and anti-Blackness disregard our very embodied humanity.

America is a raced nation. Its vision has always been a raced vision. As the late Pulitzer Prize-winning novelist Toni Morrison said, when you think of America, you think of race: it's embedded into the very definition of what it means to be an American. That's why it's so important to understand notions of Anglo-Saxon exceptionalism and white supremacy. When we talk about white supremacy, we are talking about the way whiteness has been enacted so as to negate the humanity, the personhood, the livelihood, the life of anyone else that is not raced white. When the Puritans and the Founding Fathers came over from England, thinking that England had lost its way, it wasn't as if they came to a barren land. They came over here and exterminated the Native American people. Those who weren't exterminated were put on reservations. That's how whiteness enacts itself: it's always in opposition to that which is not white. When we're talking about white supremacy, we are talking about the way it has played itself out against all the bodies of people who have not been raced white. We have seen the same thing in this country in relationship to other immigrant groups. We know the long history of the Asian Exclusionary Act, setting up virtual concentration camps in this country for Japanese Americans. We continue to see that play itself out in our current immigration policies as they have been connected to the 'Make America Great Again' vision over the last four years. We are talking about a white supremacist narrative that has not lived up to the better angels of our democratic vision.

When we have phrases like 'people of colour', or, in the UK context, 'UK minority/global majority', we have in mind some normative understanding of what it means to be human. People in the dominant cultural group, those who have been raced white, forget that they are raced. It's a funny thing that happened on the way across the ocean: you had people coming from France, people coming from Ireland, people coming from Italy, people coming from all over the European continent – and they get here and they're white. Whiteness only has any kind of content or standing when it is positioned against that which is not white. If you define the world through a grid of what is normative, then everybody else is something else. How about letting people define themselves? How about not having to lump people into a group named 'people of colour'? I want to define myself. We have a group at the centre, defining the world and how one should see the world. To talk about people as a minority, what you're really saying is that they are a minority in terms of power. We are talking about an apartheid reality. 'Minority' becomes a way of talking about the subjugated.

What we are seeing is global white supremacy. We are seeing the last death knell of people who have been used to being the colonizers and imperialists of the globe hanging on to their power. It's also happening across the European continent and in the UK. We've got to help those who are used to naming others to understand the ways in which they are raced – and that they have no priority over what it means to be simply a child of God, like everybody else.

The Make America Great Again vision that emerged in this country over the last few years is deep in its DNA. Until this country really reckons with that, we will continue to see this tug of war about the character and the essence of this country – who we want to be as a nation and as a people. It's the twenty-first-century version of the Civil War, which played out, of course, around the abolition of slavery. It continues to re-emerge because we never reckoned with it. White supremacy is the original sin of our country. When we speak of original sin, what that means is that you have a people trapped in a culture of sin. Original sin becomes generational. That's what we're seeing here. White supremacy will continue to be passed through the generations until we deal with the sin itself. So, the emergence of the Make America Great Again vision was unsurprising, especially following on the heels of our first Black president. Because in this country, any time Black people have made a modicum of progress, there's a proportional backlash. What we've seen in the last few years is clearly that backlash.

There are people who voted for this vision because they are disenfranchised in different respects. Those people also feel alienated by this nation – but unfortunately, too often, that alienation gets raced. Whatever the reason people voted for this vision, they were able to either accept or ignore its white supremacist nature. It's a privilege to be able to ignore that. What the Make America Great Again vision revealed is that the genie is out of the bottle and it's going to be hard to get it back in.

On the ballot was the character and the soul of this country. A majority of at least five million people said, 'No, that's not who we are. And that's not who we want to be.' And this is the tension. I am a 64-year-old African American woman. My great-grandmother, whom I knew, was born into slavery. And she died when I was about six or seven years old. I'm not sure if she ever got to vote. My grandparents got to vote. But they had to wait a long time. My parents, of course, voted. But not one of those people – my great grandparents, my grandparents, my parents – ever dreamt of there being an African American president. In my lifetime, I have been able to vote for a Black president. And now a Black female vice president. My son, who is a young adult – his first vote was for a Black president. His third vote was for a Black female vice president. His second vote was for an unsuccessful female president. That's the other side of this story. That's what this country can be. We have to decide which story we're going to live into. Are we going to live into a story that moves us further along the arc that bends toward justice, where all people are accepted as being created equal? On the day when the 2020 election was finally called, and Biden was declared a winner, I was actually in tears, feeling, 'Wow, I don't have to flee this country.' I felt safe again. The people decided this isn't who we are, at least for the moment. For at the same time, over 70 million people voted for the Make America Great Again vision. Nevertheless, we're talking about the change that's happened in my lifetime – the miracle that I've been able to vote for two Black persons in the highest offices of the land.

We are talking about people who are aggrieved and dispossessed, who have been marginalized and alienated from the vision. It's easy to scapegoat them and to play upon the demons of a nation. The only solution is to create a society where people are not dispossessed of their humanity. The solution is justice. In order to get there, you've got to listen to those who are dispossessed. We come from a faith tradition where justice begins with those who are on the underside of it. The only way to get toward the just society that God has promised us all is to start with those who are the least powerful. That's what framed Jesus' ministry from the very beginning. That's what his crucifixion indicates to us. When we don't do that, this is where we end up. The solution isn't to build power within an unjust system and take advantage of the divisions that injustice has created. The solution is to create a just society. And you do that by starting with the dispossessed – rather than using the grievances of the dispossessed against them. It creates divisions between those who are dispossessed, fighting for the few little crumbs of privileges that they can get within an unjust system, rather than doing something to dismantle a system that gives such undue privilege and undue penalty.

I'm a member of The Episcopal Church. The Episcopal Church emerged from the Church of England, which is the church of a colonial power. The Episcopal Church is over 90 per cent white, and that's being modest. I was born and raised in The Episcopal Church – and the Anglican Communion worldwide actually looks mostly like me. The Anglican Communion worldwide is a communion of people who are blessed with ebony grace. Again, we have to decentre Europe. Anglican is not synonymous with Anglo. Let's be clear that just because an institution calls itself church doesn't mean it's church. We always have to ask ourselves whether it's a social institution that happens to be religious or whether it's a church. Is our church aspirational? If I ask, 'Who am I accountable to?', I'm accountable to God's just future – I'm accountable to a church that is called to be an embodiment of the future God has promised us all.

Whether or not I'm blessed with ebony grace, my role in the church, as a Christian, is to hold that church accountable in its claim to be church. That's not my role simply because I'm Black in a church which is 90 per cent white; it's the role of anyone who claims to be Christian. I'm accountable for what it means to be church; I'm accountable for what it means to be a follower of Jesus. That's why our presiding bishop in this country has called us into the Jesus movement. It would help if the Anglican Communion were to heed that call and enter into the Jesus movement. This is a movement that goes through the cross. The cross and crucifixion are at the centre of our faith: I wish we would act like it. The way toward God's just future is through the cross. Solidifying our relationship to the crucified class of people will get us there.

God's love is manifest as a love that's never separated from justice. I don't think that I'm an alien in the church. It's not as if the sin of racism doesn't reside in our church, because it does. But all that means is that our church isn't yet church.

Major world religions seem to share one similar ethic at the centre, which Christians call the golden rule: do unto others as you would have them do unto you. I like to reverse that rule and say: do not withhold from another what you would not want withheld from yourself. Would you want withheld from yourself a decent place to live? Would you want withheld from yourself enough food to eat? Who would say that they would? Would you want withheld from yourself healthcare? Would you want withheld from yourself the ability to walk down the street and to birdwatch, barbecue, drive, and not be accosted? Who would say that they would? So, unity begins with the recognition of our common humanity. That common humanity begins by recognizing that those who seem so unlike you are just like you. If we can begin there, it becomes the role of faith leaders to help us, help the world, help our societies and nations broaden our moral imagination for justice. That means creating imagination that affirms that everybody that has breath and has ever had breath is a sacred child of God, because that breath came from that which is greater than us. If we can begin there, with our common humanity and with the sheer recognition that we would not withhold from another breathing soul what we would not want withheld from ourselves, then we can begin to cross divides. This isn't political. This isn't partisan. This is simply what it means to be human. This is getting back in touch with the essence of who we are: our humanity.

During the pandemic, it has inspired me to see people acting together to protect one another. There are so many things the virus has laid bare – in terms of the disproportionate ways in which it has impacted certain communities in this country, the disproportionate ways in which it has affected certain communities around the world. It has revealed that we have not appreciated the sacredness of everybody's humanity: the inequalities and the injustice. That's the sin of the world. This virus has laid that bare, even as it has forced us to recognize our global connections to one another. This virus is no respecter of borders. And the borders that we have erected – which have suggested that some people are more deserving and more human than others – have been laid bare by this virus. What has inspired me has been when the church has acted like church and led the way toward a moral response. That moral response is that we have indeed begun to protect and help and serve one another, starting with those people who are most vulnerable to this deadly pandemic. Faith communities, not simply the church, have to take the lead, but we can all do our part, simply as human beings, to take care of one another and to respond to those who are most vulnerable.

12 November 2020

8

Steve Chalke

Hope

God is love. That's the beginning, the middle and the end of the gospel of the good news. And that changes everything.

The pandemic has shaken our foundations.

It has forced us to pause.

It has called us to re-evaluate.

It has posed us some serious questions.

It has invited us to search for deeper answers.

Rahm Emanuel, the former mayor of Chicago, once declared, 'Never let a serious crisis go to waste ... it's an opportunity to do things you think you could not do before.' There is a great opportunity that arises out of this terrible moment for us all – and for the church – so long as we anchor ourselves again, in the great truth that God is love – unconditional love – for all humanity. Love, as the apostle Paul puts it, that never ends.

As for me, the pandemic has confronted Oasis – the charity I founded – with huge challenges. As we all know, this strange virus has been fundamentally unequal in its impact. It has exposed and exaggerated the deep pre-existing inequalities in our society. It has preyed on the poor and singled out the vulnerable. It has acted as a giant magnifying glass around disadvantage.

Oasis' food banks, food pantries, debt advice and legal support services, along with our community, youth and children's centres, are run off their feet. Our schools, churches and housing projects across the country have been stretched and reshaped in the work they do. And yet at the same time we have encountered remarkable new opportunities. Doors have opened that have always been shut until this point. Conversations and relationships have sprung up that just wouldn't have been possible before.

Jesus once claimed, 'I am the door.' Everybody understood what he meant. You're the entrance to something good. As a student at theological college, I was taught that what Jesus was trying to get across was that he was the 'realized eschaton'. I was never sure that I knew what that meant at the time. Now, although I think I do know, I am equally sure that few others do. And I'm convinced that Jesus won't have either. But the way that he put it was clear for all. And, for those of us who have chosen to follow him, it's equally clear how this relates to our task – to serve as opener of the door of hope. Or, for those who like to think in academic eschatological language, to demonstrate the 'now' in the 'not yet'.

The famous Greek poet named Hesiod, who lived 700 years before Christ, wrote an epic poem called *Works and Days*. The most famous part of this long poem is the story of Pandora's box. Zeus, the king of the gods, is angry because Prometheus has stolen fire from him and given it to mankind. Until then the gods had only created men. Zeus thinks that Prometheus' 'gift' has given men too much power. So, he decides to seek revenge and put humanity back in its place. And, with help from some of his colleagues, Pandora – the first ever woman – is created. Pandora is intensely beautiful, but with a heart of stone, and Zeus has a mission for her. He sends her to men with a box – Pandora's box. He orders her to open the box, out of which fly all sorts of evils – drought, famine, plague, pestilence, death and suffering. Then he orders the box to be shut, just before the last 'gift' can escape it. That last gift is hope. Hope is trapped deliberately in the box.

Before Pandora's arrival, 'man' had lived free from the 'evils' of struggle and illness. They had enjoyed the 'golden age'. But, on Zeus' command, Pandora delivered to men this terrible set of curses – but had withheld from them the hope they all needed. From then on, over the centuries that followed, it was left to Greek thinkers and philosophers to debate what it meant for hope to be locked away from humanity. People can deal with pestilence, plague and pandemics, but without hope they are lost.

The great thinker Plato developed his particular take on it all. Yes, there is hope, but not in this life. In this world – this existence – hope stays in the box. Hope belongs to the soul on the other side of death. Only as we finally escape this life can we encounter the reality of hope. If you've ever heard the 'pie in the sky when you die' gospel preached in a twenty-first-century church, it was pure Plato.

Then came Aristotle – Plato's most famous student. His view of hope was different again. For him, it is a very good job that hope is locked in the box. The availability of hope would make people lazy. Life is about effort. It is about pulling yourself up by your own bootstraps. You are self-determining. You have a responsibility to take control. Hard work liberates. But hope creates lethargy. To slightly misquote a writer of a later age – hope is the opium of the people.

It is against this background of Greek thought that the apostle Paul, the man who encountered Jesus on the road from Jerusalem to Damascus, writes. And he sees everything through a different lens. This ultra-legalistic, fiercely nationalistic, religious conservative Jew, on a mission to destroy the infant church, experiences 'a light from heaven flashing around him, blinding him'. And, whatever else it was that happened in that encounter, Saul (to use one of his Hebrew names) was transformed by it.

Paul came to understand that, through Jesus, what belonged to the age to come was breaking into the here and now – and bringing hope, not only for his own people (the Jewish nation) but for all people, all nations, all languages, all tribes, all colours and all classes; for everyone. To quote him, 'These three things remain, faith, hope and love. And the greatest of these is love.'

Why is love greater than hope? Because it is love – unconditional grace – that creates hope. Indeed, it's only this kind of love that ever creates hope.

Paul was born to Jewish parents in Tarsus – a city that enjoyed a reputation as a cultural, intellectual philosophical centre of the ancient world, alongside Alexandria and Athens. But bathed in Greek thought, as a young man, the future follower of Jesus also had opportunity to travel to Jerusalem and sit under the tutelage of Gamaliel, the great Jewish rabbi, mentioned in the New Testament. So, schooled in an understanding of hope – shaped by the mythology of Hesiod, the 'wait till after death' dualism of Plato, the pessimism of Aristotle and the Hebraic teaching of Gamaliel (who longed for the dawn of hope in the 'here and now' through the coming of a future Jewish messiah) – Paul's encounter with Jesus both transformed and completed his thinking.

God is not angry, God is love. And this love has revealed itself. Hope is not locked in the box away from humanity. In Jesus, hope has burst into our present reality. And this hope is not just for the Jewish people – a Jewish hope via a Jewish Messiah. This hope is hope for the whole world, and is therefore worth living faithfully too.

I was 14. I'd fallen in love. Her name was Mary. She went to the local posh school. I had a place at the other one! As I was often reminded: 'You're the kind of kid who'll work with your hands, not your head.' However, I discovered that every Friday night, Mary went to a youth club in the local church hall. So – using my head – I joined up too. I attended for months before my hopes were crushed. Mary, I learned, wasn't interested! Walking home that sad night, I was faced with a huge decision; the kind that jilted 14-year-olds often face. Rejected by the girl who gave my future meaning, was there any point in the rest of my life? From my school I already felt like the answer was 'no', but as I'd got to know the leaders of that Friday night club, I'd somehow absorbed their message. It was very different. 'You are created by God,' they said. 'Your life has huge potential – don't waste it.'

My mind was made up! Even if Mary didn't want me, I was going to keep going to that youth group. I liked their message, and even more their attitude. So, I was going to take up their challenge to follow Jesus – who they told me showed us how to live God's way. But more than that, I also decided that, if all this were true, my mission was to set up a school for kids who had been starved of hope, a house that would provide security for young people who had been denied love, and a hospital to lavish the care that every human deserves, but that so many are denied.

Though I had little or no understanding of what any of this really meant, I knew it was what I should spend my life doing. Only this, I somehow felt, would be a fitting response to the fact that, on this night, the view I had of myself as an irrelevance had been swept away and my life had been filled with hope.

I'm dual heritage. My father was a very dark-skinned, south Indian, trying to eke out a living in a very white south London. Growing up I knew what racial discrimination felt like, first-hand. Because of his colour, my father struggled to find the kind of skilled work of which he was capable and for which he was qualified. That meant I also knew what poverty felt like. So, the 'pie in the sky when you die' version of Christianity never did resonate with me. From the very day I became a Christian, I knew this had to change life here and now – not just for me but for others. If I had been created by the God of love, my life was significant. I was here for a purpose. My life counted for something. My future mattered. My time was not here to fritter away but to invest.

That being said, I really didn't have a clue what I was talking about, but in my early twenties I trained as a Baptist minister. It was, after all, a Baptist church that ran that wonderful youth group. And, after working as an assistant minister in a local church for four years, in 1985 I started setting up the first little pieces of a charity to get the job I had done.

With some help from Cornelia, who was by then my wife (I met her at that same church youth club), we set up a house in Peckham, South London, which we still run, and which gives shelter and care to vulnerable young women. Cornelia suggested that we should call it Oasis, because it would be a place of hope and refreshment in the barren desert of life. That's how Oasis got its name – though funnily enough, we never did give the house that name, because slowly we worked out that, for anyone who was coming to live there, the last thing they wanted to do was live in Oasis towers or hostels. But the charity did become known as Oasis – with a goal always to create places where hope is tangible.

Since then, Oasis has grown; our mission wherever we work, in the UK or elsewhere in the world, to build and to help others build, strong, inclusive local communities filled with hope – tangible hope – where every person can find their place, flourish and achieve their God-given potential. As part of that, we have gone on to develop significant housing stock for vulnerable people, a number of churches, a huge variety of health and community projects, and a family of schools – both primary and secondary – with over 32,000 children. All of this introduces me to many conversations around child education and welfare.

I have a friend called Dave. He is a vicar in North London. He tells the story of how a woman joined his church. She came from a completely non-churchy background. And he happened to overhear one day – in the coffee shop his church ran – some people, who had wandered in, ask her a question as she sat there: 'So are you a Christian now, then?' They waited for her response. Her answer was brilliant. 'Well, I couldn't say. I guess you'd have to ask my friends here to tell you if they think I am or not.' She got something important very right in that response, didn't she?

Being a Christian, a follower of Christ, isn't a label – a noun – we attach to ourselves. It's a way of living. It's a way of being. It's a way of doing. A way of bringing hope. Jesus says, time after time after time, 84 times in the four Gospels, 'Follow me.' Follow me. I am the way. I am the truth. I am the life. This is the way to live. This is the truth. Bask in it, enjoy it, don't settle for anything else. Live this way. Celebrate this way of being. Walk this way.

So, taking that theology and putting it into practice, within Oasis, we talk about the 'Nine Habits' – better known to you as the 'fruit of the Spirit'. What we say to all our staff. To everyone. To those from Christian, Sikh, Hindu, Muslim, atheist and all sorts of other backgrounds, we say that these habits sit at the core of Oasis – defined by the life, teaching and example of Jesus. It is this that drives everything we are and do.

Over the years, we've constructed our induction programmes and leadership development around exactly this. So, whether you're joining Oasis as a CEO or an apprentice, you begin with the same introduction course. And our continual professional development – training for junior leaders, middle leaders, aspiring senior leaders, senior leaders, regional and national leaders – is all based around the same nine habits.

These, as we always say, aren't themes we sat around in a focus group to come up with a few years ago. Instead, Paul the apostle, who encountered Jesus in that life-transforming experience, writes to some of his friends in a region called Galatia. We know his letter as the book of Galatians now. In this letter Paul describes the traits of Jesus' character – which, using a metaphor, he calls the fruit of living in tune with the Spirit of God.

All we've done is take those nine character traits and rebrand them as the Oasis Nine Habits.

And, we have found this. That it is the people in the ring, the people with skin in the game, that find they have voice in the big societal discussions. When you've got skin in the game, then people ask your opinion. And, more than that, also find that they are given new and bigger opportunities. When people trust you, new doors open themselves up to you.

In the last few months, the Children's Commissioner, Anne Longfield, has talked about the cliff edge facing many of the most vulnerable children in our society, while Amanda Spielman, the Chief Inspector of Ofsted, has been saying that because of the pandemic, we are looking at a whole generation of lost young people. We know that there are huge numbers of children and young people who are persistently absent from school at the moment – ghost children, as they are sometimes called. Children falling out of school, into exploitation and even criminalization.

Or, what about the tens of thousands of children who have not had a bedroom and a laptop and warmth and food and security and coaching and support through the pandemic? How will they 'catch up'? They're disturbed. They're traumatized. They're anxious. They've lost their desire for life. The stuffing has been knocked out of them. Their long-term futures are compromised. They are living without hope for the future.

Because of this, within Oasis, we've been talking together about how we develop an approach and a set of educational innovations that work for every child. How do we stop any child falling over that cliff edge? How do government, local churches, schools, the justice system and other agencies all work together to prevent this disaster?

At another level, all part of this same issue, we've recently been asked by the Ministry of Justice to launch the UK's first Secure School, a therapeutic alternative to a youth jail, for 14–17-year-olds. We believe that this will mark a revolution in the youth justice system. It is all about the justice system catching up with what we've learned about brain science in the last 30 years. To that end, a new piece of legislation is heading through Parliament, which will also make it possible, for the first time in British history, for a charity to run a custodial estate. That charity is Oasis – and Oasis Restore, as we will call the Secure School, is designed to be the proof of concept, that a system built around a trauma-informed and neuro-aware approach works.

All our staff – youth workers, teachers and health professionals – will be specially trained to work with these children, who are often dangerous to themselves as well as to others. And, once again, this training will be based on and around Oasis' Nine Habits.

We are going to work with children who've been sentenced to us by a court. But, for the most part, they are in the justice system because of the failure of other systems: education, social services, health, housing, youth work, policing, along with the closure of children's and Sure Start centres. Their sentencing comes at the end of this long chain of system failures. Equally as bad, the incidence of reoffending among teenagers, once they leave custodial care, currently stands at 69 per cent in the first year. An even deeper scandal is that Black children are overrepresented in the system, alongside those who have been 'in care' and those who are neuro-diverse etc. These kids have been dumped. The systems that they should have been able to rely on have failed them.

That's why we've named our Secure School Oasis Restore. It will operate based on an underlying theology and philosophy of restoration rather than of retribution. You can't help someone by harming them. Oasis Restore will provide a sanctuary that offers security, rather than a jail that deals in punishment. Our residents will be students, not offenders. They will live in houses, not on wings, and they will sleep in bedrooms rather than cells. Society has a long history of punishing the psychologically wounded. But we all know that it doesn't work. We will not do it. Rather, the core principle that will drive our work is relentless love – and the gift of healing hope and a sustainable future that accompanies it.

Using a metaphor from William Booth, the founder of the Salvation Army, if you spend your life fishing people out of the river they are drowning in, by throwing safety lines and pulling them to dry land, that's social action. But, if you have any sense, eventually you're going to wake up and say, 'Why don't we wander up-river and work out why all these people are falling in? Let's build a bridge.' That is social justice. The task of the church is never simply to fish people out of the river, important as that is, but always to work to build the bridges to stop them falling in, in the first place.

The theologian N. T. Wright wrote that although Christians tend to think that Jesus was a preacher, in fact he was a politician. Jesus did things, extraordinary things, provocative things. Things that made people sit up and take notice. And he sometimes stopped and commented.

I grew up in Croydon, and I remember standing at a bus stop and reading the advert on the shelter. It was a few weeks before the local elections were due to take place. The ad read like this: 'Question: What takes just two minutes, but lasts four years?' And then at the bottom, was written, 'Answer: Your vote!' What a thin, shallow misunderstanding of politics or democracy. We vote for the kind of society we want, with our actions and our involvement, every day of our lives.

People sometimes ask me, 'Have you ever thought of going into politics?', by which they mean, 'Do you want to become a local councillor, an MP, or perhaps join the House of Lords?' Well, here's the thing. I am in politics. We're all in politics. The term 'politics' comes from the word *polis*, which simply means the city. Thus politics refers to the affairs of the city, the affairs of the community. And, we all have an important, grass-roots level, role to play in the affairs of both our local communities and in society as a whole.

'Love your neighbour as you love yourself,' said Jesus. 'Love your enemy,' he dared to comment on another occasion. That is a deeply political statement – and when followed through on is an even greater political act. Every follower of Jesus has the same calling. We are in the business of getting hope out of the box. We're here to carry hope into our communities.

I still live in South London, and sometimes I run along the South Bank of the Thames – I pass St Thomas's Hospital and the Florence Nightingale Museum. I marvel at the number of church spires. The architecture of my city is shaped by the hard work and the faithfulness of the church in previous generations. But the question I contemplate as I run, is how we – the twenty-first-century followers of Jesus – will continue to create doors of opportunity, justice and inclusion for our generation. Or, put differently, how do we tell the world that hope is out of the box – right here, right now.

10 December 2020

9

Michael Curry

Community

I think there's a call to those of us who are church, who seek to follow Jesus of Nazareth and his teachings and his spirit and way of life as our way of life and love, a call to go beyond where we have been. I've said to our bishops, over and over again, the day will come when we'll re-enter the churches again, but don't leave the congregations we've discovered online – don't leave them behind. Don't necessarily expect that they have to come through the physical doors of the church. I don't know what it's all going to look like, but we've been pushed into something that on the one hand was occasioned by hardship, but on the other hand may well prove to be a blessing: to be in conversation and relationship with people who might never darken the doors of our church, for a variety of reasons.

There's another thing I've got to tell you, and this is personal, but I think it's true for others. I'm not sure that I've ever been where I am so vividly aware of Michael Curry's need for God and human community. Now, that's not to say that I wasn't aware of it before. But there's been something about experiencing the absence of incarnate physical human church community: even when it gets on my nerves there's something about it, something about experiencing and knowing God in gathered community, even when you want to pull your hair out. There was a Broadway show called *Your Arms Too Short to Box with God*. I don't have the spiritual musculature to do this on my own. And it isn't only my arrogance that would think that I could. When I was 25, I actually thought I could, but at 67 I don't even remotely think that any more. But there's something about this pandemic, and the realities of our limitations, as well as our giftedness, that it has made me aware of how much I need God. We need God for real, and we need each other. And that may be a deeper calling that will result from this: a realization of who we are as followers of Jesus of Nazareth in the community that we call church; that there's a real need for anything that draws us closer to God and the love of God into each other and love for each other.

I have long contended that the opposite of love is not hate. The opposite of authentic love is selfishness, self-centredness. Love is the antidote, it's the corrective to that. It is selflessness and discovering the true self. There's a libertarian streak that is deep in the American soil. There's a famous flag with a curled-up snake that says, 'Don't tread on me.' The further you go west, the bigger that rugged individualism becomes. This is the culture of Horatio Alger's rugged individualism, and that's utter nonsense. The truth is, it can degenerate. Instead of the energy that makes one want to achieve and improve, which is positive, it can degenerate into self-centredness. It is nothing but selfishness writ large. It's not only been in not wearing face masks. Some of the most grievous offenders have been churches that have, in spite of government pleadings, gathered large numbers of people together to worship. There's not an Episcopal church doing that, I'm happy to say, but we've had to say over and over again, 'Love your neighbour as yourself means put on a face mask.' That's what it means to love your neighbour. If you care about somebody else besides yourself, wear a face mask.

Actually, there was some discussion among the medical folk. Now they're saying you need to wear the face mask to protect others. But the truth is, you need to wear the face mask to protect yourself. And the doctor who said it said maybe that will be a more appealing argument to some people. Maybe appealing to altruism isn't good enough. The truth is, there's a disguised greed, selfishness and self-centredness that is behind much of this. And some of it has come out in this pandemic here in this country, so that wearing a face mask becomes a political statement. It's maddening. It's self-defeating. That has been fostered by political agents, President Trump and others, to the detriment of the culture we've got. It's spreading like wildfire: the virus is out of control here. I hope they'll get the vaccine out and get it going fast enough. But it's going to take that to really bring that readiness in. And it's because part of it is due to unbridled selfishness.

That's where I'm going to be very honest. Just as William James wrote the book *The Varieties of Religious Experience*, there are varieties of Christianity. There's a way of being Christian that looks something like Jesus of Nazareth, it looks something like the parable of the Good Samaritan, something like the Sermon on the Mount, something like the command to love God and your neighbour itself. And there's a way of being Christian that looks like wearing a face mask, a way of being Christian that is simply about me and God and my getting to heaven. That stark variety and differentiation has become clearer and clearer. And I don't say that from a position of self-righteousness. It's agonizing to say that; but it's the reality. I think at the root of it is selfishness.

Nobody tells me what to do. You don't matter to me that much. And we've seen it in the attack on our Capitol last week. I don't want to say libertarian, because there's a healthy streak in libertarianism and I don't want to cover everyone. But it is a kind of libertarianism that is rugged, pure individualism, that is unhealthy and socially destructive.

The first thing I would tell Joe Biden as he takes office is that, of all the presidents, we have to pay attention to Abraham Lincoln. Pay attention to his first inaugural address and his second inaugural address in what he said and did. He had to do some things that he didn't want to do, but he had to do them for the good. His ultimate goal was to bind up the brokenness, eventually – but he had a civil war to fight. And so you have both to work to bind up the wounds, do everything you can to bring people together to be in relationship across differences, to be able to debate and to deliberate, and not to shoot and to agitate to be able to do that. And at the same time, you've got to get vaccine in people's arms, you've got to get this virus under control, you've got to make sure that the kids that are out of our public schools, most of whom are the poor, will not have to go without meals, if they don't have free meals from school. The schools are figuring out ways to get them their food, but you've got to get the schools back running again, get kids fed again; you've got to create the social safety net underneath people.

If we're a humane, compassionate and just society then we should get Congress to get people the money that they need, so they can eat until they can get jobs again. This is not about philosophy. This is about humanity. Joe Biden knows that. I'm not telling him anything he doesn't know. But he's got to do two things at once. He's got to do some healing things. And he's got to do some pure humanitarian things that will take care of people until they can take care of themselves. And if anybody can do it, he's the right person for the right time. Religion speaks here. He needs to model a way of being a person of faith that is humane and kind and just and decent and grounded in love. He can model that. And that could be a reformation for us.

Ultimately, some things have to happen before healing really begins. To be sure. But you do them at the same time. I was one of the heads of the various communions that signed a public letter last week, calling for President Trump to resign for the good of the nation so that it could begin to heal and, if he didn't resign, for the 25th amendment to be enacted, and if that wouldn't be enacted, for the President to be impeached and removed from office, even if he was no longer physically in office. It's not the greatest letter, but it says pretty clearly that in order for this nation to heal, we have to face up to wrongs that have been done. You can't just skip from a night of wrong and jump to daylight. It doesn't work that way. You don't get to Easter without Good Friday. It's like Frederick Douglass here in the nineteenth century, in the movement to end slavery, so that people who want freedom and justice without agitation and without struggle are like people who want crops without ploughing up the ground. They want a harvest without the thunder, the roar of thunder, the flash of lightning and the pouring of rain. The reality is, we have to face what we have done wrong, what has been wrong; we have to name it and face it; we have to have truth, as they could teach us from South Africa. That becomes the prelude or sets the stage for the kind of healing and reconciliation that eventually brings people together.

That's what Abraham Lincoln needed. This was a man who had to fight the Civil War, and at the same time let us bind up our wounds. I love this country. All of my uncles fought in the Second World War, and they fought in segregated Black units. But they did it because they believed in America, not in what America was doing all the time, not in its hypocrisy, but in its ideals of freedom, justice and equality. And they were willing to give their lives for that. That's what I mean. And going back to Joe Biden, hopefully I'll get a chance at some point to be in a room with him. It'd probably be with a bunch of clergy, so you get a lot of sermons, but I'd like to say it's those ideals and those values that are worth sacrificing for, because they can make human life humane and liveable. And from my perspective, they resemble what Desmond Tutu and others call the dream of God, and God's vision for a beloved community on this earth.

The perplexing piece is that a significant number of people have believed a lie. And no facts seem to alter that belief. Even to the point of not wearing a face mask, not believing that the virus is real and dangerous. I'm not sure I know how to counteract that, except that an alternative national narrative is created from the top. But they've got to see it; it's going to take time, but they've got to see it. They've got to see the kindness of Joe Biden. And the firmness to be as he must. He's kind. And he's a tough politician. He's where Jesus says, 'Be as wise as serpents, and as innocent as doves.' Martin Luther King had a sermon called 'A Tough Mind and a Tender Heart' – you got to have both. He actually does. Another narrative could be created.

The other thing that has to happen, we've got to foster intentional relationships across difference. And that is hard to do. We struggle with that in the church. But we've got to do it. One of the things that has led to the fragmentation in the United States Congress, the House of Representatives and the Senate, is that back in the 1990s, there was a move to detach people from being in relationships across different political parties. And then people started going back home on weekends, so they weren't actually living in Washington and going to church together – going to bar mitzvahs on Saturdays, going to confirmations on Sundays, going to baptisms – and they were no longer having the human relationships that actually create community that has the potential to handle diversity and difference. So we've got to have some intentional way of doing it: groups like Braver Angels,[3] working with former senator John Danforth and some others, and Adam Hamilton from the United Methodist Church now working together to see if we can create intentional ways that bring people of difference together. There's got to be that kind of thing, as well as changing the national narrative. And I believe we do have to have something that takes the insights of the methodologies of Truth and Reconciliation and creates a national conversation.

Insurrection at the Capitol of the United States! I never thought I'd live to see that. I lived through Jim Crow segregation. I never expected to see what we saw last week, but it happened. Maybe we can take that horrendous negative reality and crack it open and create a national discussion about who we are, and who we seek to be. And that's going to take some work. And some of the learnings of truth and reconciliation are that you've got to name some stuff. Some of the support that Donald Trump has received has come from people who have been left out, put down, looked down on by the intellectual establishment and intellectual power centres, and forgotten. There's a reason they've been raging and crying out. They don't have a voice. And instead of finding a constructive voice, they found the voice of demagoguery. And you know what, if sheep don't graze, if you don't give them a loan to graze on, they go and graze on something and it may not be good. And that's partially what's happened.

It may well be part of the failure of a liberal democracy to really be genuinely inclusive, including our rural communities, including people who are afraid the economy is changing. You may know this in the UK, too. Ways of earning a living are not the same. I grew up when it was steel mills and stuff. Well, that stuff's gone or not, it doesn't exist in the same way. I grew up in Buffalo, New York, where steel was how people made their living. Now, it's high tech and medicine. Those are the companies, and if you don't have an education you are left behind. And you're angry. And the liberal Democrats aren't answering your needs. And along comes somebody who says, 'I'm going to make it right for you', even though he's lying. So that's got to be addressed. Joe Biden comes from that world. And maybe he has a chance to change the narrative through actions and words that could help.

---

3 Braver Angels is a citizens' organization uniting Democrat and Republican Americans in a working alliance to depolarize America.

We have got a lot of work to do: to bind this society, to heal it and to right its wrongs. What happened to George Floyd has been happening since I was a little boy. It's been happening since Emmett Till[4] in the 1950s. It's been happening since there was lynching in the whole first half of the twentieth century. I was on Zoom with some indigenous Native American leaders in the church just last week. We were meeting and talking about this exact same thing. They talked about learning how to survive hardship, and learning how spiritual values can help you endure difficulty. They said, 'We were removed from our land. We've experienced genocide, we've lived through being relegated to the reservations. We've lived through the indignity of what's happened to us. And yet we have still sent our young men off to fight in the military, and they're proud to carry that flag.' Listen to them. Just listen. There are dispossessed people all over this country. And some of them are the people who turned to Donald Trump for help, because nobody else was helping them.

You know what? Somehow we've got to get close to the Jesus of the New Testament, not the Jesus of our culture. The Jesus of the New Testament. I was part of a movement that was called Reclaiming Jesus, which included Jim Wallis from Sojurners. He said, it's very interesting that many of our Christian voices sound religious, but they never talk about Jesus in the Sermon on the Mount. They don't say a word about the Beatitudes. They don't say a word about loving your enemy, they don't say a word about Matthew 25, the great day of judgement, when what God is really concerned about is, 'Did you feed me when I was hungry and clothe me?' They don't say a word about that. What happened to the Jesus who said, 'The Spirit of the Lord is upon me, because he's anointed me to preach good news to the poor'? What happened to the Jesus of the parable of the good Samaritan? What happened to the Jesus of the Gospels? They avoid that Jesus like the plague, and talk about everything else, and it sounds religious. But it ain't got nothing to do with religion. It's ideology, disguised as theology, which sounds like religion. So we've got to reclaim Jesus – the Jesus of the New Testament, the Jesus of the Gospels. Go there, wrestle with that Jesus of Nazareth, and then let's talk about what Christianity looks like. So I start there.

But the other thing is, we've got to demythologize Christianity itself. And I say that as a lifelong Christian, and somebody who is a Christian. I believe in this stuff. I really do believe this stuff. And I believe it makes a difference. I've seen it make a difference. To demythologize Christianity

---

4 Emmett Till was a 14-year-old African American boy who was abducted, tortured and lynched in Mississippi in 1955, after being accused of offending a white woman in her family's grocery shop.

itself means to swipe away all the myths that have gotten added on to it. I mean, the myths of culture and civilization, and ways of being Christian, which have altered the picture of the New Testament Jesus. If it doesn't look like Jesus, if it doesn't love like Jesus, if it doesn't care about others like Jesus, if it doesn't long for a relationship with Abba Father like Jesus, it may well not be Christian.

I tell the bishops all the time: if they don't act like Jesus and don't look like Jesus – don't do it. And that's not a partisan position. Jesus had a way of getting along with folk, all stripes and types. He wanted to know, did you love somebody? Did you help somebody? If I can help somebody along the way, then my living will not be in vain. That's what Jesus was talking about. And that's what got him in trouble. Got him killed. Jesus got killed because of the kind of world that he was talking about. He got killed because he loved people who didn't want to be loved. He cared for people. He actually cared about hurting folk and poor folk. And he said, that's our family and we've got to take care of each other.

The civil rights movement here in this country, in its earliest days, was deeply grounded in the life and teachings of Jesus. In 1963 Dr King wrote up ten commandments as part of the training manual that was used for training non-violent resisters in the Birmingham campaign, and they were principles for how a non-violent resister acts. The goal of non-violence is not revenge. It is justice; but its ultimate goal is reconciliation.

We must always speak and act and think and talk in the manner of love: for God is love. It's principles like that. But the first one is, before you march, meditate on the life and teachings of Jesus. What was new was the Spirit of Jesus of Nazareth. It was not an exclusive Spirit. It said, 'Come unto me, all ye who are weary and heavy laden.' That's the Spirit of Jesus. That Spirit had to inhabit our spirits, to love our enemies, even as we seek justice, to change the structures, to change the system – but to love even the perpetuators of the system. He said to do that, the human spirit needs to comingle with the Spirit of Jesus. As Kelly Brown Douglas would say, 'You've got to demythologize Christianity, and get down to where the nitty meets the gritty – get down to the essence and the core of Jesus of Nazareth.' And there, I'm telling you, there is a living faith.

Jesus establishes the precedent of what it looks like to follow him. It looks like to live a life consistent with God. That's what you see in the Acts of the Apostles. They weren't pretty all the time. But they inspired themselves to become an inclusive community of Jew and Gentile. They discovered all of a sudden that what they thought was the case, might not, in God's mind, have been the case for their time. There is nothing more stunning than the Gentile inclusion into the Christian movement. Because it was basically an Emancipation Proclamation, it was a declaration of independence. It was equality, freedom and brother- and sisterhood declared for all of God's children, all of God's people. Paul in Galatians says something stunning: 'For all who have been baptized into Christ and put on Christ, there is no longer slave or free, no longer male or female, no more Jew or Greek, but all are one in Christ.' This is a way of saying, we are one human family. In spite of all of our antagonisms and problems and issues, God has meant us to be a human community, a community with all of God's creation. That's God's dream and God's vision: for us all to find a way to live together as God's family. When we do that, we can overcome any nightmare. They wouldn't have come up with that on their own. Jesus was already signalling the gospel. The Spirit took them and said, 'Now, here's a little bit of what it looks like. You don't want to do it. But I'm gonna take you and make you do it. Anyway, Paul, you don't want to go to Rome, but you're going to get there anyway. You're not a St Peter, you don't want to do some things. But you're gonna do them anyway. The Spirit is gonna take us where we don't want to go.' It's like Jesus of the Last Supper in John's Gospel saying, there are many more things that I could have told you, but you can't handle them. I love that passage. But the Spirit of Truth will lead you into all truth. I really believe that about us as the church. God is bigger than Christianity. God is bigger than the church.

When Dr King began in Montgomery he did not know that it would have implications for the whole country. They didn't realize until years later that it had implications for the world. What started out was about race, between Black and white in the South. Wait a minute, this includes the Native American folk. Wait a minute, this includes Latino and Hispanic folks. Wait a minute, this includes women. Wait a minute, this includes LGBTQ folks. That's what the Spirit will always do. And we don't control that Spirit. We don't have control. That's God. God is the great emancipator, because God is free.

Remember when the Macedonian called? They wanted to go one way, and the angel said, 'Now y'all can go over there, and then you want to go another way.' And another angel said, 'No, you can't go over here.' And the Spirit of Jesus wouldn't let them go over there. And then they saw a man from Macedonia, who said, 'Come on over here, it is the spirit of Jesus that will lead us to the beloved community.' Which is what God had in mind when God said, 'Let there be.'

There's an underground Harriet Tubman movement, which is the real Jesus movement. And it's in the church. And it's in the world too. People who are in that movement are people who have said, 'I'm going to live a life that looks something like Jesus. I'm going to let the Spirit take me, and I'm going to be a part of a community that can help me to do that.

Because I don't have the strength by myself, all on my own.' Find those folks, and walk with them.

I've gotten in a little bit of trouble here. I believe in unselfish evangelism – which is to say, the purpose of evangelism is not to repopulate our churches. The purpose of evangelism is to help folk find the God who created us, and made love in us; and to nurture a relationship with that God, which is loving, liberating and life-giving in relationship with each other. And if the church happens to get blessed in that process, fine. But if another way of faith gets blessed, fine.

Don't give up on the quest. Or on fellow pilgrims, because they're there. I love the church. Because I do believe that the Jesus movement is here. I don't mean that it's everywhere, because it's not. It's sometimes in cells with people. I know that – I've been a pastor long enough. But I'm telling you, if there are saints in Caesar's household, as it says in the New Testament, trust me, there are even saints in the church. Sometimes they're not loud. And you have to listen for them. Because they're real quiet.

I remember there was a woman in the congregation at St Andrew's Church in Hall River, North Carolina. You can't get more country than Hall River, North Carolina. She found out that when kids in foster care who were in the public schools had a birthday, no one was bringing in little cupcakes to celebrate. She just said, 'We can make sure every child has a birthday party.' And she started baking cupcakes for kids. That little church of about 75 people joined her. That's a Jesus movement that smells like a Jesus movement. There are people who have sacrificed greatly for the cause of love in this world. And some of them are in the church. And some of them are not. You've got to be in community with them, be in fellowship with them. Because you need them, and they need you. Maybe they're not in the formal church. Maybe they're in another gathering. But get with them. And then then read up about this Jesus and listen to him.

When I first became a bishop, I had a spiritual director who at some point said to me, 'Ask yourself, "Why was I elected?" I don't mean in terms of popularity or of what the people who elected you were fully conscious of. Why you? There are other people smarter and cuter than you are. So why, why you?' What was it from my story that meets this story that may help the Jesus story? Kamala Harris's story is of a little Black girl with an Indian mother and a Jamaican father. She somehow brings Asia and Africa together in America. Her parents met doing civil rights work. She's a Baptist, but she's also a Hindu. What was it about you Kamala? Like in Esther, you have been chosen for such a time as this. You thought diversity was just Black and white together. Oh, no, I'm gonna show you some diversity. This is God's diversity. And I'm gonna bring a whole bunch of the Indian community in America who are just as proud as they could be right now. Nobody has been thinking about them in the United States because their numbers are small. But nope, not any more. Because there's a girl named Kamala. I would say there, what does the Spirit have in mind for you? And that gives you the mission. We say 'e pluribus unum' is the motto of the United States of America: from many, one. Are you are being called to help to make that real? We just have a small part to play. It's part of God's great design and desire for the beloved community to be the dream that gets realized in the new creation.

We ask our gracious and loving God to make this world one where all are cared for, all are loved, all are cherished, and justice is truly done; where the hungry are fed, children are loved, and every man, woman and child, no matter who they are, where they are from, no matter their race, their religion, their class, their country, no matter their wealth, or poverty, their sexual orientation – that all of us are seen by each other as we are seen by you, as your children, as brothers, sisters and siblings. And, like the old slaves used to say: walk together, children, and don't you get weary, because there's a great camp meeting in the promised land.

God love you. God bless you. And may God hold us all in those almighty hands of love.

14 January 2021

10

Sarah Coakley

Evolution

I can't just talk about the pandemic – because living in America through the last paroxysms of Trump's presidency has made it perfectly clear that whatever I say about the pandemic has to be coiled together with the way recent months have ripped the top off systemic racism in this country. One can't fail to notice that this mega-crisis is drawing attention to all our difficulties in living together in this country and in the world. Underlying this is the threat of cosmological and ecological disaster – and the economic and social and political structures which keep us from being able to perceive how these interrelate, what we need to do about it, and what we're *able* to do about it.

There's a film I've watched three times now since this crisis began. It's one of the best ways of getting into the structures of American racism. The film is called *I Am Not Your Negro* by James Baldwin, the great African American writer. The film proceeds by first lamenting and reflecting on the assassinations of three of Baldwin's friends, younger than him: Medgar Evers, Malcolm X and Martin Luther King. But it goes on from there to say that what Baldwin was really worried about was not only the fate of African Americans in America, but the 'soul' of America itself. He shows that the narratives of hegemony, power, freedom and unity are built on the systematic denial of the rights of certain 'other' people. What has to be set off against the miracle of uniting all these extraordinarily disparate people into one country, under one flag and under one rule of life, is that the underdog becomes unseen. Baldwin ends the film by saying, 'If America didn't have the Negro, it would have had to invent the Negro.' The immediate challenge now, not just in America but particularly in America, is to do the inner spiritual work that allows people to reflect afresh on how they are implicated in the 'racialized' political and economic conditions which prevail in this country, and which, right now, still prevent many Black people from flourishing as they have a right to hope to.

It's easy to miss these dynamics if you are working in the academy. Since the civil rights movement in the late 1960s, most universities have at least made attempts to include people who otherwise might be dis-advantaged. But in a place like Harvard, where I taught for 15 years, this admirable effort distracts one from what is going on just down the road in Boston, a city which has rather little opportunity, even now, for Black people to become middle class. It wasn't until I served in a jail as I was training for ordained ministry that I was able to see my own whiteness through the lens of mass incarceration occurring in South Boston. This has now become better known through the work of people like Michelle Alexander, who has pointed out since 2010, when her book *The New Jim Crow* was originally published, that many of the promises of the civil rights movement were shut down under the rubric of the 'war on crime' – because the war on crime was actually a war on the Black civilian. And this was when the yet greater intensification of police brutality and frisking in Black areas came to a new climax under a 'liberal' mandate of seeking out the drug dealers.

You also have to probe what is happening in the church. The white churches in America have historically used their prayer and their wor-ship – 'unconsciously', of course – as a further bulwark in the systemic maintenance of racism. For instance, the number of genuinely interracial congregations in The Episcopal Church in Washington DC is still tiny. I've been lucky to serve one in the last year. And that's been enormously stretching and interesting for me.

I've been thinking a lot, too, about the question of evolution. For some decades now (specifically since the discovery of 'genes' and their role in evolution), an evolutionary narrative put forward by some leading scientists has argued that the story that evolution delivers to us is one in which selfishness is the only successful undertaking. By now, people tend to take this 'neo-Darwinian' story about our 'genes' for granted. It's been so well propounded by excellent popularist science writers that it's difficult to peel away the metaphysic and ethic that has become entangled with the actual scientific investigation. It's become hard to ask: wait a minute, is that what *Darwin* said? Is it what he meant or envisaged? And is that the only way of interpreting all the new information we now have from the genome?

I don't think it's a coincidence at all, to weave in another metanarrative, that in the same period we have experienced, across the globe, a pre-dominant form of neoliberal economics – a particular manifestation of capitalism. I'm not myself anti-capitalist, *tout court*. What I'm concerned about are the global forms of economic capitalism that have taken hold since approximately 1980. Looking back, we can see that this was the moment when the economies of developed Western countries ceased to be closely connected to the gross national product of each country, and became forms of banking manoeuvre – indeed, of online 'betting' as a banking manoeuvre. This was of course abetted by new developments in the computerization of economic and banking life. If you look at the story that evolutionary theorists were telling us at this same time, and you compare that with the story that the economists were telling us, they can be seen to have had curiously parallel developments. In fact, there was a moment in the middle of the Enron scandal when the person in the dock justified his nefarious behaviours by reference to the 'selfish gene', as if that story of evolutionary anthropology were the justifying fundament of a particular way of behaving in the economic markets and in business. (Dawkins himself, incidentally, was extremely embarrassed by this saga.)

How do we throw a new light on these cultural developments, which seem to have become so familiar as to be unquestioned? This seems to me to be the great challenge at the moment: to link how we think about evolution with how we think about our economy in relation to politics, recognizing that so much politics has *become* economics. (And that's another development that's occurred in this time.) And this, of course, is in turn deeply entangled with the stories of Covid and the stories of racism – here we have the big picture which all thinking people, and certainly all thinking Christians, ought to be concerned about. My own work for my Gifford Lectures arose from a fascinating three years spent with mathematical evolutionary biologists, looking at how the investigation of the evolutionary phenomenon of 'cooperation' has undermined some of that selfish gene ideology at its base. It's not that evolutionary biologists now say there is no 'selfishness', no competitiveness, no viciousness, no 'nature red in tooth and claw' in evolution. But that has always been counterbalanced by another factor in evolution that we're now beginning to understand mathematically. Evolutionary populations all have the capacity for forms of cooperation, in a technical sense – not just as collaboration, but behaviours which are 'sacrificial' with positive results for the whole population; some part of the population loses out genetically, but the whole population benefits as a result.

This is particularly exciting in the realm of ants, as E. O. Wilson charted with such significance. In the realm of animals, meerkats are supreme cooperators. They're probably even better than humans. Chimpanzees are pretty good at it too. Whales and dolphins are amazing. We're beginning to understand more deeply how these factors balance one another and make for either the flourishing of communities and populations or their gradual decline (of course there are interactions here not only within one 'population' but with other species and with prevailing conditions, including weather conditions). This raises fascinating questions for ethics and, indeed, for theology. What if it turns out we're 'hardwired' for cooperation in order to flourish *together*? What new light might that throw on Jesus' teaching in the Sermon on the Mount? This is fascinating stuff. I think the generic significance of evolutionary cooperation is still not generally known out there in the public world, because, as with any scientific paradigm shift, scientists hold on to their old paradigm ferociously before they're willing to give it up.

Turning to the pandemic, then, the first question that must be asked is this: on what economic theory are you basing the presumption that everybody has to risk their lives to get out there and keep working? Because there are alternatives – such as reconceiving how we work together (which we've already done to a significant extent), prioritizing safety for those who are risking their lives because otherwise they can't put bread on the table or because we who don't have to go out can't live without their sacrificial behaviours. This is where the matter of cooperation really bites – the apparent clash of medical safety on the one hand and economic expansion on the other. I don't hear many people offering an alternative paradigm. It would involve a shift to the left in most countries – if the highest priority were to protect and sustain people, to make sure that they were able to eat and that the vaccine was disseminated in a way that was genuinely democratic, favouring those who most needed to look after others. That's not really happening in the United States (to say the least). My husband went to get his first vaccine last week and when he came back I asked him how many non-white people were in the queue. And he said, 'Funny you should ask that. I only saw about two.' Some states are better than others on this matter, and we know how Republican politics and states have affected the distribution of the vaccine and attitudes towards it. There's nothing apolitical about this crisis, and anything that is political is also economic.

Another writer who has been really helping me at this time is David Marquand, an economic historian, who a few years ago wrote a book called *Mammon's Kingdom*, about Britain after the 2008 crash. He made the point that after the international economic crash in 1929, the world *changed* its economic views. There was the 'New Deal', there was Keynesianism to inform it, and people eventually recovered with the sense of a new horizon of hope. After the 2008 crash, in contrast, everyone was meant just to look the other way. The bankers who had brought this upon us were in some cases berated and lost their jobs, but in other cases just carried on while the state had to pick up the bill. We all did, in fact. But there was no real renegotiation of the economic status quo. It's remarkable. We've got time now to think about this.

As an academic, I have a vested interest in the dissemination of information – the creation of new ways of thinking that might help us to make some prophetic turns. We need people who are able to write across disciplines. One of the problems in contemporary academic life, and in political life, is that we don't have the necessary detailed knowledge of all the disciplines that we need to bring to the table to solve this particular crisis, in all its vicissitudes. But on the evolutionary scale, there are things to be learned from this moment – about what we have done to affect ecology and animal populations – which some people think created the conditions for this virus to jump out of various animal species into the human. We then have to look at how this virus has been disseminated. This is extremely closely related to the way we travel and the degree of communication we have across countries – and therefore the ease with which this pandemic has spread, compared historically with earlier 'plagues'.

We need the evolutionary virology perspectives. But we also need the political perspectives, because unless we collaborate, or 'cooperate' even sacrificially, in the sharing of information about the medical amelioration of the disease itself and its treatment and prevention – which, by the way, I think we are doing quite unexpectedly well; this is the bright side of the story – then we're also stuck. This in turn presents us with one of the biggest problems for contemporary democracies. That is, you can't make major changes that affect long-term human behaviours in relation to pandemics and ecology in the space of a very short four-year government. So, this is a crisis of Western democracy, because it's never in the interests of a prime minister or president who doesn't have a very large majority to start making demands – in relation to taxes or emissions or whatever will make it difficult for him or her to stay in power. We come up against what we came up against after the First World War and the Second World War: that we need international forms of communication and cooperation, and the power in them to make changes, without which we're going to founder. In fact, we have to go back to the story about cooperation and its human forms; we have to extend our amazing international communication to face this multifaceted crisis together. And I think this is the biggest moral challenge that humanity has ever faced: it's literally a matter of life and death.

When the United Nations was formed, there was no internet. We can communicate with each other now, and not just at the level of the higher elites, in ways that we've never been able to do before. And this has all happened in my lifetime. When I gave my Gifford Lectures, I ended on a slightly depressing note about how difficult it was politically for anyone who understood the importance of cooperation to make it work now and globally for the sake of ecological survival. Several young people who attended the lectures who were scientists and not Christians (and I was delighted that they came to the lectures at all) got back to me afterwards. And they said, 'We actually do have the technical means of communication to do this work. But the question is, how do we form the political alliances across governments, whether they be democratic or not?' One of the great ironies here, of course, is that some of the non-democratic governments are doing much better at facing this immediate *disease* problem than we are – precisely because they're communists. That's not an argument, as such, for communism, but it does tell you something about how the emergency responses to something like the pandemic can be easier in more authoritarian political systems, if they are working for the sake of the people.

I'm not a natural economist. But this is an area in which I'm now starting to read intensively because anyone who doesn't is likely to have the wool pulled over their eyes by our politicians. We need to ask: what are our fundamental assumptions in economic theory? How do we justify them? And what are the alternatives? David Marquand, for instance, is strongly in favour of returning to a Keynesian set of presumptions. I've been thinking about William Temple and his extraordinarily prophetic work, after the First World War and into the Second World War (during which he died). He wasn't ashamed openly to be a member of the Labour Party; he wasn't ashamed to be a friend of Keynes. In his great, very short, book, *Christianity and the Social Order*, he set out a vision for our country – which I think our current religious leaders are afraid to do, whether for fear of loss of support or just for lack of information. I think churches like St Martin-in-the-Fields, which sets such a prophetic bar in the United Kingdom, should be enabling the articulation of these big economic questions. I think it's our (and your) duty.

It's sometimes said that economics is the new theology. Some indeed would say theology itself has become entranced and stupefied by the reduction of politics to economics. But I think what I'm increasingly learning is that political theology and economic theology is what's needed at this time. What's required is the reimagination of the possibility of a culture that is truly and deeply Christian, and which obeys the commands of Jesus' most difficult teachings. That means sharing sacrificially with others – and sharing is not popular. It's not mandated culturally. What's mandated culturally, both by the neo-Darwinian evolutionary story we've been told of late, and by the economic story, is that you should strive to the top for yourself and your own – and if that means (negatively) sacrificing others, that's just the unavoidable outcome.

The 'eschatological' card (as theologians call it: that which relates to the final theological 'end') can be used in both directions. It could, for instance, be used to justify serfdom in Tsarist Russia, because it was assumed that the peasants would get their reward *after* death. That's eschatology as political deferral, which I would argue is a debasement of Christian eschatology. But if all we have is now, then we can't have hope at all. And hope is absolutely key to long-term projects that may actually change the world as we know it. And thus it's integral to what I'm trying to argue: because I believe 'science' is now capable of delivering a vision of forms of intentional, sacrificial behaviour for the sake of the whole – which can be seen, in retrospect, to have flavoured positively the entire creative development of evolution from bacteria up. And of course, theology has to deliver the message about what goes *with* this insight humanly, which is that the ultimate motivation and sustenance and graced capacity to cooperate comes from our faith. Our faith, our hope and our love hang together. Of course, the greatest theological virtue is love. But without hope and faith, 'love' can seem thin, pale and sentimental.

Many people in our current culture, including, of course, Christians, are suffering deeply as a result of their health, grief over lost loved ones, and through the widespread mental health issues that this state of affairs creates in us. But I'd like to think of this time as an enforced and lengthy *retreat*, a period in the wilderness where we're being asked to do some very deep inner work. Christians can show the way here – and the church ought to be guiding this undertaking. This inner work is neither narcissistic nor elitist. It's the work that we all ought to be doing as Christians all the time. But now we have the opportunity to do it. More seriously and intentionally. It's prophetic work. Go back to the great crises of the Second World War and think of people like Dietrich Bonhoeffer, resisting Nazism, or Mahatma Gandhi, campaigning for independence in India. What they saw, and which I think our contemporary church now finds it very difficult to understand, is that the deeper the call to inner work, the more profound the political ramifications. It's not a disjunctive choice.

Unfortunately, we've created a lot of recent trends in 'spirituality' which are really about narcissism and self-development, not about facing these big moral questions we've been discussing. The church thus has a prophetic role here in calling people to reconsider what church fundamentally *is* – in terms of the discomforting 'interruption' of the Spirit, calling us into a new way of thinking about ourselves as community and in relationship to the world. Another point follows from that: out of that wellspring of newly developed repentance and transformation comes the prophetic voice itself. But the church is by and large letting us down in that regard. Its leaders are mainly concerned about loss of finance and where and when churches will have to close. How much panic is caused by the fact that people can't meet and can't hug each other and therefore can't reassure each other? I'm not downplaying those anxieties. But if we, as a church, concentrate on that and not on what the positive spiritual outcome of all this current travail could be, then not only are we losing our moment, but we're losing our sense of what it means to be followers of Jesus.

There's a prevailing anxiety that has gripped the church in recent years. Rowan Williams constantly reminds us that you never do anything really positive for the church out of anxiety. Unless our gathering together to worship can evoke the transcendent – not only the great spiritual comfort but the *challenge* of the transcendent – then we're no better off than anyone else in tackling key political questions. In fact, we may be worse off, because we're using the church to protect us and cocoon ourselves against the realities. That's what white Christianity has done classically in the United States. In sustaining racism in America, it's used church, it's used prayer, it's even used the Eucharist for those purposes. If our main concern is the number of bodies that cross the threshold, rather than the extent to which we are growing and deepening spiritually, then we have lost the basic Christian plot. That doesn't mean that we should fall back into wallowing in hopelessness. And, on the other side, I'm not sneering about 'evangelical' ambitions to missionary expansion – quite the opposite. That's exactly what we need. The question is: how do we combine strong apologetics, evangelical expansion, training and formation in the Christian faith with a strong sensibility that we have a responsibility as Christians to *grow* spiritually? How do we avoid using the church as a buffer *against* our own growth, an option which is always so unconsciously seductive?

In the Sermon on the Mount, Jesus asked us to do at least six impossible things – whether 'before breakfast' or any time (consider again Matthew 5.21–48). Reflecting again on what these challenges might mean in the life of grace and sanctification does and should continue to discomfort us, along with Jesus' many remarkable parables about *money*. It is so astonishing that so many of his sayings and parables are about money; so few are about sex. Each one of them has a strange punchline that you don't expect: the most peculiar being the Lucan parable of the dishonest steward (Luke 16.1–13). Meanwhile, Paul gives us his extraordinary vision in Romans 8 of a cosmos that is yearning towards completion through the suffering, death and resurrection of Christ. He says we can only access that through that unique and disconcerting 'interruption' of the Holy Spirit in our prayer (Romans 8.26). This whole chapter in Romans is also the one great passage in the New Testament about ecology and the implications for the natural cosmos of Christ's death and resurrection. It's about our being bound together in Christ, not just to each other in the church but to all creatures, as we now know we are. This is the great vision of the body of Christ, in which we are all interdependent and rely on one another – a vision of cooperation that comes with sacrificial cost.

Then there's 1 John on sin (1 John 1.8), which links to the man born blind and John's Gospel (chapter 9). I'm so aware of how sin is connected with perceptual distortion. A deep feature of sin is an incapacity to see what's right in front of our noses. We need to think very seriously about how it disables us. It's a matter, though (the nature and origin of sin), on which the Christian church has never had a unanimous view. What are its outcomes? And how are Christ's death and resurrection and the giving of the Spirit the means of its progressive undoing? What do we have to offer here to a world that can't perceive how it's killing itself?

We've heard a lot of late, especially in the UK, about the phrase 'private prayer' – the one thing you're allowed to do in a church during the pandemic. But there is a current cultural presumption that private prayer is some sort of navel-gazing. However, even if such a practice is discomforting, it's discomforting in the same way that psychoanalysis is discomforting: it's for the expansion of my psyche. But one of the great things about the adventure of silent prayer, of all prayer, when you allow it to go to any depth, is that when you start in on this great adventure, it seems terribly lonely: down, down, you go and all this garbage inside you jumps up and hits you in the face. You think, 'I'm alone. I'm in great danger. My world is shaking.' But the further down you go, the more you see that this is the least private thing you do, even though ostensibly you do it by yourself. But it's what links you at the most profound level to each other, through a transformed consciousness and a transformed set of priorities and goals.

I've been accused of not having a sufficiently sophisticated theology of grace. But my theology is characterized instead by a very strong emphasis on pneumatology, on the doctrine of the Holy Spirit, and nothing could have delighted me more than the *Journal of Pentecostal Studies* wanting to have an issue interrelating with me about the work I was doing. I don't think there's ever any genuine renewal in the church without a renewal of reflection on (or rather, submission to) the work of the Holy Spirit. The translation of the word *paraclētos* as 'comforter' of the Spirit in John's Gospel is misleading. What it really means is 'one called in to help'. If we're in discomfort in the church, that's a good sign. We *should* be uncomfortable. We should be asking for the Spirit's help. The question is: what are we being asked to do in response to the Spirit – not only in terms of our own growth, but in terms of giving hope to the desperations of the world and to the future of our cosmic ecology, which, after all, is the most dangerous crisis of all among the ones we're facing.

11 February 2021

11

Jonathan Tran

Materiality

I am a philosophical theologian in Waco, Texas. We're in the central part of Texas, what's often referred to as the heart of Texas (which comes with the apropos acronym, HOT). Waco is a really great place, although not a place my family and I ever thought we would end up. I grew up in Southern California, having migrated to America from Vietnam after the American war with Vietnam ended in 1975. I came to Christianity right before college, and the question then – and now – is whether any of it is true. For me the evidence for whether it's true is whether the church ends up being what scripture portrays it being. That is, if the church exemplifies the Spirit's work in the world, then the church should look like what scripture seems to suggest. If that's the evidence I'm looking for, then you might imagine I go back and forth on this question, given the church's wildly uneven witness. To me, the faithfulness of the church is where the rubber meets the road on any number of questions I take up as a philosophical theologian.

I'm a Vietnamese American. The American war in Vietnam is effectively the first war that America 'lost'. American history is largely told by its history of wars: the Revolutionary War, the Civil War, the two world wars – all wars America won. It's a story told through war, and it's a story told through wars won. Telling its story as progressive winning allows Americans to narrate its future as if always on the right side of history, such that its actions get read as the actions of winners, the cause of justice, progress, inevitability and so on. How then do you continue to tell the story of America through a war lost? Does that fundamentally shift how Americans understand themselves? That's the great challenge the Vietnam War presented to Americans. If you've been to Washington DC and seen the Vietnam Veterans Memorial, it's an extraordinary memorial, mainly for its ambiguity. It looks like a literal wound on the earth, like someone took a huge knife and tore open the earth, like an open wound. How do we tell that story? The contested history around that memorial reflects the contested story of Vietnamese Americans. What do we represent to America? Do we represent its failure? Its imperial ambitions? Do we Vietnamese Americans, in so far as we've achieved 'model minority' status, represent its redemption?

Immediately following the war, America decided to allow 120,000 Vietnamese refugees into the country, my extended family among them. And I could tell, growing up, that Americans had no idea what to do with me or my family, just as they had very little idea what to do with the war. Do we represent a moment of redemption in so far as we are here, in so far as we have become American, in some cases poster children of the American Dream? Or do we represent a moment of failure? That set of questions opens up to a larger set of questions about the moral character of this country, about its past and what that past says about its future.

I'm aware that, in America, I very well fit what's been called the 'model minority'. I'm not simply a minority, but a picture of how minorities should be. We come to this country, we work hard, we keep our heads down, which means we don't complain, and we achieve levels of success, like getting a PhD at Duke University. That's largely the script that was presented to me. The other members of my family are all college edu-cated and pretty successful people. Hence the 'model' imagery. But the reality is a much more complex picture. South-East Asians are among the least college-educated ethnic group in the United States. Cambodian Americans have one of the lowest high school graduation rates. I came over when I was three, early enough to be shaped to the specific contours of American culture, pliable to the American Dream. Now imagine some-one who came over when they were ten, with experiences of war, gangs, drugs and all the challenges that come with that, relationally, socially, educationally, etc. These are pretty common narratives among large swathes of Asian America, but these are not often the stories told when people think about Asian Americans. Americans would rather mytholo-gize a model minority, which allows them to think the American Dream is alive and well, even carrying the face of a Vietnamese war refugee. Yet, these lesser-known minority reports tell a different story. For me and my siblings, that was certainly the case.

My family came from wealth. They grew up in North Vietnam. When the communists took over and dispossessed the landed classes of their wealth, they became poor. Coming from wealth and power, they had little idea how to negotiate poverty and powerlessness, which wasn't part of their experience. So when they forcibly migrated to the south and later came to America as poor war refugees, these were tough times. I moved 14 times before I got to high school, migrating in and out of cycles of poverty. I didn't become a Christian until right before I went to uni-versity. But the church was a significant presence in our family's life, because one of the ways the US government figured as a way to assimilate Vietnamese migrants was to put them in churches. So the Episcopal Church, the United Methodist Church, the Presbyterians all adopted Vietnamese migrant families. Our family was adopted by a Lutheran family. Personally, I got very little out of that experience since I was just too young. But it did leave some indelible marks.

My first memory in life was when I was about five years old. We had been in the country just a couple years, and my brother David and I were crossing the street – he was six and I was five at the time. He was hit by a car and was killed. Those images of us crossing the street and him getting killed are etched on my brain, making for an extraordinary first memory. The other thing I remember about that time is the church coming around my mother. I'm sure they shared very little culturally, even very little language. But I recall their presence to our family. It's those kinds of things that, even if I couldn't put much of it together, became part of the witness of the church that made me think maybe there is something here. The church, even though I was not a Christian, then became part of a script of a very particular Asian American story, which is to say, a particular American story.

So much of the Christian faith revolves around the second person of the Trinity – Christ, the full expression of God's investment in the world or, more simply, God's love for the world. The material reality of that investment is the church as the material witness of Christ. Theologically, different churches work out in different ways how we locate the presence of Christ in the community called the church.

While there's a fair amount of Catholicism in Vietnam, that wasn't our culture as a family. I grew up in a world pretty devoid of divinity, at least so far as we knew. There was the Lutheran Church I mentioned, and the way those Christians wrapped their arms around my family after David's death. Amazing as they were, they didn't play any kind of imaginative role for us; it would not be through the church that we would imagine our American lives. The default position for us then as it is for me now is 'No God'. Given that I grew up that way, only later becoming a Christian, my life is now this constant negotiation between what I have come to believe and the default position I was raised in: God or No God. Those for whom the default is God, those raised in faith, can forget how different things are if raised otherwise, how much of a leap faith in God involves. That's why the church matters so much to me, because it evidences, or not, what scripture and the traditions of Christian faith claim about God. Who God is depends on who Christ is, and who Christ is depends to a frightening degree on the church actually being the church. If the church is not in some significant way the church enlivened by God, then we have good reason not to believe in God. In the Old Testament, faith in God was covenantally validated through things like children and land. God's existence for the Hebrews looked like something, required something, embodied something, and hence formed the inescapable materiality, bodiliness, of Jewish faith. Similarly, Christ comes to us materially through the sacraments of the church. Just as it is Christ who makes God known, so the church makes God known, the incarnate body of Christ given in the gathered body of Christ. The church is not the only way God makes Godself known, but it is the way the New Testament doubles down on, thereby serving as a criterion for discerning God elsewise in the world.

Christians tend to want to play fast and loose with this connection between witness and belief, as if Christian faith can survive indefinitely in the face of reasons for unbelief, which surely the church's many moral failures present. And one can imagine why, because the church is often pretty horrible, and that horribleness elicits reasons to not believe. If it is true that Christian faithfulness provides reasons for belief, then Christian unfaithfulness provides reasons for unbelief. Witness and belief, given the incarnational/covenantal shape of Christian belief, are inextricably tied in this way. Philosophically, it's easier to divorce the connection than to commit to it. But this is precisely what incarnation and covenant don't allow. And the New Testament certainly gives very little room for a disconnect between witness and belief. There, Christ and church are materially connected. Amazingly, the New Testament presents this inextricable relation as good news, reminding us that no matter how bad we can be, how unworthy of further investment and love, God will do all that needs to be done, take all the time in eternity, to make us a faithful people. So we always have the capacity to be better than we are. The deep connection between witness and belief sounds like an indictment of the church, and it is that, but it is also a promise of what the church is, has been and can be. It's true that if we're not faithful, it's not clear that Christ exists. But it is likewise true that in so far as the Spirit enables us, we always have this capacity to express God, and reasons for belief in God, in the world. It's always at hand. It's a matter of laying claim through our lives to the revolution wrought in Christ.

If I'm trying to resist too easy a division between Christ and the church, I'm also trying to imagine them together and in a way that actual churches bear great importance. People often think that the primary meaning of baptism is its relationship to individual salvation, that is, baptism has to do with my being saved. That is no doubt part of how the theological tradition read through scripture has understood baptism. But baptism also says something about community and about one's communal belonging, that one belongs to Christ and Christ's people. Another way of working out the connection is to say that salvation *looks* like something, and that something takes communal form, that baptism initiates one into corporate salvation. Baptism is an intensification and an individuation of what nature always already is as participant in the life of God. What baptism does is intensify and illuminate all of that for the individual. It says to the individual, you are part of what God is doing in the entire universe in saving the world. It's not so much that your life *ought* to reflect that, although it certainly should. It's more that in so far as your salvation comes in Christ it already does, in so far as you've been baptized into Christ's crucified and resurrected body. One of the things I'm interested in pressing theologically is the idea that Christian faithfulness, while it's an impossible task – losing our lives to follow Jesus – is also the most natural thing we do. In so far as we exist at all we exist as God's grace, such that living godly lives is the most natural thing we do, who we were created to be. It's sin that's artificial, something parasitic on a more natural mode of existence. We ought not to think that giving our lives for God and for others is somehow a strange thing. It's what we were created to do. It's what it means to be a creature – to reflect the gift-structure of our lives, of all existence.

I'm a Christian. My whole life depends on the church being what scripture says about it, both in its frailty and in its goodness, truth and beauty. I can never claim the church's beatitude about myself, though I have friends and the church has saints, whose faithfulness at least intimates the beatific vision. But I would like to think that what my life amounts to, what any Christian life amounts to, approaches in some small way what the apostle Paul means when he says claiming resurrection risks foolishness, lives that only make sense if Christ is in fact raised from the dead. I would like to think I'm inclined in that direction, though with fits and starts all along the way.

Being Vietnamese American is certainly part of who I am. We live in a time where racial identity is supposed to tell you everything about who you are. I've been racialized in a very particular way, as an Asian American. But what that means is highly ambiguous, as is the nature of race and racial identity themselves.

I've been committed to issues of race reconciliation, diversity and anti-racism my entire life. I had to be. I grew up at a time when racism was not only accepted, it was expected. You would walk down the street, and you would get it from whoever, whether it be white folks or other folks. It didn't serve anyone by saying, 'Well, I'm not actually, I'm not Chinese': that missed the point. It was just constant racism. And so I've always been kind of committed to this, mainly as a form of survival, or at least a way of making sense of my own life and history. A few years ago, I was asked to write a book on American racism and Christianity from an Asian American perspective. And the proper way to do that would be to take the reigning discourse around race, racism and Christianity, and just expand out its edges in order to include people like me. This would be a similar project for someone in America who is Hispanic or Latinx – say, Mexican American. The idea is you take the standing concepts and ideas about what race and racism are, and just push it out a little bit in order to include others. You diversify the diversity discourse.

What I realized as I drilled down on the literature and came to see its limitations, and reflected on how those limitations did or didn't make sense of my own experiences, was the sense that anti-racism marginalizes those already marginalized by racism. There's a way of talking about these things that presumes that a certain way of thinking about race works for everyone. You just expand the categories. I found that to be painfully untrue. Not only that, but there's ways that this worked out politically, that the more we committed to the way we talked about race, the more people like me simply would not matter or, worse, would look suspicious or even perilous. And if we did matter, we would always matter in a kind of secondary way. So that was part of the realization that there's something wrong. But that wasn't the primary problem. The issue for me wasn't trying to get greater representation for non-white or non-Black people. The bigger issue for me was whether that way of thinking would ever get us to actual justice, to actual liberation.

If the goal of anti-racism is justice and liberation, I found that the current discourse was just going to further corner us, putting justice and liberation beyond reach. These corners, at least in the American context, are becoming increasingly contested around issues of race identity. So my goal was to think outside this, or beyond it, or through it, by rethinking what we mean by race and racism. It became a massive project. It's the attempt to step back, get behind the curtain, and look at how we've gotten to where we are, and at what remaining resources there are. One way I characterize the task before us is to recognize that race and racism name extraordinarily complex realities, and to ask whether or not we possess the moral vocabulary, the concepts and arguments sufficiently complex for taking in those realities and getting us closer to justice and liberation. This is where Christianity really matters to me, because it has a very sophisticated moral vocabulary. We can think about these things in ways that can help us expand our imagination and thinking through these questions.

My book *Asian Americans and the Spirit of Racial Capitalism* involves a bit of oral history and a bit of ethnographic study. It begins by showing that the theories for race and racism we already had, those focused on racial identity as the principle of analysis, were collapsing under their own contradictions. To think about race as a phenomenon between, say, white and Black people, as it's almost entirely thought about in America, is to collapse under the contradictions internal to race as a concept. My context, as an Asian American, puts enormous pressures on that conceptual apparatus, laying bear the contradictions. And yet we are, in America, wedded to the white/Black binary. What I was trying to do was get behind that and figure out why that's the case.

I read a comment this morning from your Prince William, while he was defending the Royals from a certain controversy, that the royal family most certainly isn't racist. And I think about how such declarations usually function, the work they are doing or are trying to do. There was another sort of story that came out the same week, about an American basketball player who was caught on a hot mic yelling out racist slurs about Jewish folks. Or another story, the same day I believe, about the trial of Derek Chauvin, the man who killed George Floyd, or part of the group of men who did. When we think about these various cases, each mired in complexities, in the narrow terms of race identity, the question is going to be, 'Is the royal family racist?' 'Is Derek Chauvin racist?' 'Is this basketball player racist?' Once you have boiled down complex cases into platitudinal analyses of the kind 'Is X racist?', then you enter into a set of rather familiar procedures: we try to trace out the evidence for the racism; we look at the Twitter feeds; we examine what kinds of things they read online, the kinds of things they've said. The procedures – their calling out, cancelling and virtue signalling – are predicated on this idea: if we can search out the core racism, as if racism exists as a kind of box inside the individual's head – maybe it comes with a big red R – then we can say we have identified the racism, found the racist, and by identifying them have removed them and enacted justice.

But this is too narrow a set of questions, too banal a set of procedures, based on too reductive an account of racism. Instead of asking the question about who the individual racist is, and how we can identify him, we need to ask much broader questions about the structures and systems that benefit racism. I find it helpful to ask people to ask themselves a simple question: if it's almost universally agreed upon at this point that racism is bad, why does it persist? We would like to think it's a matter of tracing down people's internal racist intents and ideas, that the racism in the UK and the United States and all across the world is somehow the result of people having bad ideas, poor stereotypes about people, their colours, and so on. That is entirely too convenient a story. It's too easy to think that what happened with officer Derek Chauvin was that he possessed racist intent and because of that killed George Floyd, as if he went to work that day looking to kill a Black person. With racial identity as the principle of analysis and with this reductive account of racism, it becomes about identifying and cancelling individual racists, hopefully before they do harm, but most certainly after. And this is a familiar procedure, one caught up in how we think about Officer Chauvin and about the British Royals, as to whether or not they are racists, about that basketball player in relationship to Jewish people. Once we have found the racist, identified the racism, the next step in the procedure is to punish, to scapegoat the sacrificial lamb, with the intended effect of laying blame squarely on this individual while leaving untouched the larger society, which depends on these exculpatory procedures. The larger society, in which racism is at work, makes use of individual racists and for that reason produces them. That society goes on.

A much harder conversation is, 'Why do we think using police and prisons is going to help us deal with the extraordinary realities of inequality and injustice? Why are we dealing with effects and not causes? What do we gain by scapegoating the police, individual police officers, while leaving intact, even strengthening, a society where we use police to police the poverty we create?' That's a much more difficult conversation to have, asking those questions. It's much easier to scapegoat Derek Chauvin, and to place on his head and the heads of the other three officers the weight of American racism and its political economic constitution. The reality is we have structures and systems that go back hundreds of years, which racism helps facilitate. Racism is not some individual thing existing in some individuals alone. Racism is systemic justification for dominating modes of exploitation, and has existed only since the beginning of the US experience, but very much birthed the US experience.

Take for instance American chattel slavery. We often think something like this (and this is again part of the problematic, overly convenient way of thinking about things): Americans or Brits enslaved Africans because we were confused. We didn't think they were human. And in that confusion, we accidentally enslaved them. That's the story we tell ourselves, and we can see why because it puts some distance between that horrible past and the present, between slavers and us. We narrate slavery as if it were a massive category mistake, a collective confusion about the ontological status of persons; we thought they weren't human but, thank God, we corrected that mistake and now treat them as humans. In fact, the truth of the matter is that, in enslaving, we knew full well that enslaved persons were human. The entire system of slavery, how it worked and its built-in processes and commitments, which included living intimate life alongside enslaved people, was predicated on their humanness, on their powers and abilities as humans, of the intimate knowledge that these were human people and not, say, animals or automata. Entire structures of American chattel slavery were predicated in the deep humanness of slaves, which was there for all to see. It wasn't that we made a category mistake and therefore treated those who are human as less than human. The tragedy is that we dehumanized those we could not fail to know were human. That's the tragedy. That's a much more difficult moral reality to come to grips with, a much more complex reality, itself dependent on complex moral psychologies, than the easier story about ontological confusions.

It's similar with Derek Chauvin and George Floyd. It's much harder to think about the structures and systems that led to Mr Floyd's death and much easier to scapegoat Officer Chauvin. Without that harder story, without that deeper analysis, we end up in those conflicted corners I talked about earlier, where our anti-racism collapses under the weight of its internal contradictions. In the case of Chauvin, we find ourselves cheering at a guilty verdict, applauding the very same criminal justice system that uses countless Chauvins to unjustly incarcerate thousands of George Floyds. In these corners, we live these contradictions without so much as noticing.

So we need a much bigger story than the ones we tell about race and racism. While questions like, 'Are the Royals racist?' 'Is this or that basketball player racist?' are important, you can imagine how they become diversionary. They divert our attention from the structures and systems we need to address, because we turn to narrow stories about racial identity and individual racism that allow us to divert our attention, to turn our heads away.

My book, where I try to work all of this out, *Asian Americans and the Spirit of Racial Capitalism*, is divided into two large studies of actual communities who put all of this on display. The first is an amazing history about Chinese migrant workers who were brought to the American South after the Civil War, during the period of American history known as Reconstruction. Chinese and subcontinent Indian folks were being brought to the UK, the West Indies, the Caribbean, for many years as experiments in indentured labour. These Chinese folks were brought to the South to replace emancipated slaves in the cotton industry that existed between Manhattan, Mississippi and Manchester. They were brought specifically to the Delta region of the Mississippi river. The Mississippi Delta, one of the most fertile places on earth, was central to the global cotton industry. The economic dominance of the UK and US relied on very cheap or enslaved labour to harvest all of the Delta's cotton during this period known as 'second slavery'. After emancipation, plantation owners brought in the Chinese as replacement labour, hoping for economic conditions that would, like slavery, keep a global economy based on cotton dominant. The Chinese migrants caught wind of what was happening and refused this arrangement. But they remained in the South. They then built a life for themselves over the next hundred years in the Deep South, what some people refer to as 'the most Southern place on earth'.

These Chinese people, some of America's first Asian Americans, developed a business model that became extraordinarily successful. They became the wealthiest Chinese Americans in the country. And, incidentally, per capita the most Christian. What I look at is the way their Christianity feeds their business practices, which are directly exploitative of their Black neighbours. That's the awful backstory of how Christianity feeds into racial violence, a story where the Christianity does nothing for the cause of justice, and, in fact, just the opposite. Christianity in this case was so deeply divided from material life, as if Christianity had nothing to do with how we treated our neighbours, how we made and spent money, our employment or labour practices, our systems of profit, and so on. Acting like the mirror opposite of our reductive accounts of racism, this picture of Christianity imagines something individual, private, internal, fixated on accounts of salvation as personal and baptism as having nothing to do with concrete communities. I interviewed a bunch of these Chinese American Christian folks in the Delta, I read tons of archival histories, and over and over again you see these Chinese American Christians trained in a brand of Protestant Christianity that taught that racism hasn't much to do with Christianity – much less did their business practices have anything to do with anything of moral or spiritual significance.

The much more positive side is the second half of the book, where during the Covid-19 pandemic I was able to be online for many hours each week for a year and a half with an extraordinary church in San Francisco called Redeemer Community Church. It's a church that was founded about 20 years ago, by a number of college graduates, a number of whom were from Stanford University, one of the most elite universities in America. As university students at InterVarsity Christian Fellowship, they learned about racism and poverty, and about Christian responsibilities along these lines. They learned through the American evangelical civil rights leader John Perkins about redistribution, relocation and reconciliation. And they gave their lives to radical economic reparations. Using their Stanford brains and training, they've created a multiracial, multigenerational church. Eventually, people quit their previous jobs and created a software company with the purpose of creating a socially responsible business that would redistribute money. In the same way the tech industry across the world has led to revolutionary changes in how we do business, technology and social relationships, the Redeemer Christians asked, 'How can we harness that same ability to resource local communities and neighbourhoods?' So they created a company called Dayspring Partners.

The crucial thing they do is redistribute the money they make in the local community. This is a software company that tries to relocate the money it makes in one of the most impoverished marginalized parts of San Francisco. They have created a neighbourhood school to educate the kids in the neighbourhood – who, because it's marginalized, tend to be African Americans, Latinx kids and very poor Asian immigrants. The average tuition for private school in San Francisco is quite high. It's near US$50,000 per child. Here's a way to educate kids in their neighbourhood for US$2000 a year. It's a way for local parents to buy into it. They do this by redistributing income.

Their amazing community practices are matched by amazing practices within their company. For example, in the US, the CEO in top companies makes on average 287 times as much as the median worker – that's not the lowest worker, just the median worker. At Dayspring Partners, the CEO is committed to never making more than three times the lowest paid worker, including the custodial staff in their company. This creates a humane work environment, one given to much more democratic forms of governance.

None of this is particularly novel to the way the church in general works. What's really amazing about the church has always been its redistributive economic acts: it's always about the Spirit's gathering of people, and Christ redistributing grace to a graceless world. And with that redistribution of grace and salvation comes a material redistribution. So it's an amazing church community.

Most of us on the outside of a community like Redeemer are going to look at what's amazing about the church in its micro-economic practices, or what it's doing in the neighbourhood with the school. But what's equally important about this church is that everything it does begins with its communal life, with worship in the church, as a church, its liturgy and all those things that Sam Wells and Stanley Hauerwas have been on about for a couple of decades now. This is where everything begins. It's this communal life, of committing to one another, of being accountable to one another, of being intentional about who I hang out with and how I spend my money, how I think about people who are different from me. It's this baseline communal reality that is the beginning of everything else they do. It's them laying claim to what is already there. In this, Redeemer illumines ontological realities all around us – in fact hardwired into creation. The structures of reconciliation are both built into creation as a kind of form of self-repair and have been powerfully brought forward through Christ's ministry. This makes Redeemer folks simultaneously some of the most amazing human beings one will come across, and the most ordinary. They're laying claim to what is already there – what the Spirit is already doing.

When I say that race and racism are justification for economic exploitation, what I mean is that you have systems of domination going on and, to make them seem natural, instead of talking about the structures or the domination and exploitation, you create fictions of race, and you use those fictions to blame the victims. You say, 'You are to blame for your domination and exploitation; it's because that's who you are, what you are, natural to you, something about your race.' So morally you could get away with enslaving or exploiting Chinese workers in the nineteenth century because that's who they are as yellow-race workers. Race makes us think that it's something natural to them that gives way to this kind of exploitation. It's a distortion of the natural – and it's just pure ideology. It lies on top of the structures of exploitation to give those structures a veneer of respectability. It's deeply unnatural to treat human beings this way. It's profoundly artificial to persons and communities. Only the ideology slapped on top makes it seem like a natural thing, a moral thing, a responsible and reasonable thing. This is one of the things that we most have to highlight as much as we can: the structures of exploitation are all across the earth, and they rely on systems of ideology to justify themselves. They're clearly demonstrated in the case of American chattel slavery.

The liberative bit of good news in all this is that those who are exploited, no matter the ideological identities slapped on to justify and distract from justification, share something in common. It's a natural inheritance of all who have been oppressed by these systems to discover that they share so much with other oppressed people. And this is important because part of the ideologies is to pit oppressed people against each other, using oppressed people as scapegoats of other oppressed people. But a liberative moment arises when oppressed people say, 'We're not going to believe the lies that tell us that there's something essential about us racially. That's what we need to resist. And we're not going to believe the lies that separate us from others striving for liberation.'

My book argues that rather than thinking about racism in terms of racial identities, those ideologies used to justify dominative exploitation and pit us against each other, we need to think about political economies as those systems of ideology that facilitate domination, exploitation and division. Only when we see how everything hangs together political-economically, and how race is situated in that, will we see what's really happening to us and around us. Then will we find sightlines towards liberation. But as long as we remain committed to this racial identity that's been unnaturally imposed upon us, we're going to be stuck in a conceptual corner.

To be clear, liberation from race-based domination and exploitation doesn't mean something like colour-blindness, or post-racialism or any of those silly popular notions. We have to keep clear about how oppression happens. And this requires that we keep on the table some notion of racial identity so we can trace back the dominative exploitation. But just as we have to keep race on the table to trace back lines of oppression, we have to be very careful about how we deploy it. We need to be extremely cautious that in talking about race when talking about racism that we do not give new life to race as a concept of humans. We need to handle race as an idea, knowing that we have a tendency to essentialize people, to reduce them to race, and in ways that will further facilitate domination and exploitation.

Even our best laid anti-racist plans have this tendency, and I see this in lots of talk about 'whiteness' and 'white fragility'. There we rightly seek to identify how white supremacy works, but we talk about white racial identity in ways that tell white people that the most important thing about them is that they are white. This not only reprises race essentialism but it instantiates what white people have been telling themselves for too long, that their whiteness matters most. What if instead we reminded white people that their being white is a fiction fabricated to lend them power over others, and that, evacuated of that power, 'whiteness' is a silly myth and one they should run from?

The question of what we mean by race runs into questions of what we mean by humanness. Getting to this requires an account of human creaturely ecology, an ecology of the natural orders of our existence. The baseline of all creaturely existence is the Trinitarian life of God. All creatures exist in ecologies within that larger ecology. If the baseline ecology of all existence is God's grace, and if the terms of that grace in the context of sin are justice and mercy, then the most natural thing in the world is justice and mercy. They are natural to the world because they are natural to God, because God as a God of justice and mercy created and sustains the world. And so in claiming justice and mercy, I'm not claiming some imaginary script that's being imposed on the hard reality of the world. I'm laying claim to what is true about the world. A story like this makes evident any lies set against justice and mercy. The thick truth of God's justice and mercy makes a lie of the thin ideologies of race and dominative exploitation.

What I find beautiful about the Redeemer community is that they participate in a micro-ecology between this church, the school and the business. But that ecology exists also within an ecology of that part of San Francisco Bayview-Hunters Point, which exists within a larger trans-global, transnational ecology. But all of that exists within the ecology of God's life. This is what I mean by saying that what Redeemer does is the most natural thing in the world. Living as Redeemer does is the proper extension of living within God's life of love.

That's one of the reasons racism is such a destructive reality. It's a distortion of that natural ordering of things; it's a lie about how God has ordered the world. People have made destructive use of that in ways that created extraordinary structures and systems that benefit very few at the expense of the vast majority of human beings. And as we're learning now, as we've been learning over the last decades, at an extraordinary cost to the rest of the earth. Reversing that will entail reclaiming these natural connections between us and all that is not us, which includes other humans, other creatures and most certainly God.

The reigning anti-racist orthodoxy is what I describe in the book as identitarianism. It means people who construe various issues where race is the primary principle of analysis. Here we think about racism using narrow concepts of racial identity rather than thinking broadly about the political economies that use race – what I call following the Black radical tradition, 'racial capitalism'. Let me give you an example. A huge issue is the issue of gentrification. The story of gentrification is often narrowly told as being about racial identities: white people moving in on Black people and Black communities. If you tell the story this way, then it seems the primary driver is white people as white people. They're evil, they are possessed, it's essential to who they are, etc. The identitarian explanation is that white people are possessed of their whiteness, of some essential quality about who they are as white people that makes them want to do these things. Once you have this story, everything else goes out the window since race is meant to explain everything. Once you have that story on board, no one talks about how property relationships are managed in cities, about the connections between local, state and federal governments, about how permits are negotiated, and so on. Rarely then does the identitarian story involve low-income families facing systems where governments allow exploitative practices towards their employees, real-life stories about income disparities or about how wealth outpaces market growth. Rarely is a story told about the modes of political dis-enfranchisement that sets up gentrification, or about how governments do not enable collectivization or local forms of organizing and political power. It all becomes about the race.

And for white people, it all becomes about them being white. The whiteness description is an entirely too convenient way of describing this, just like scapegoating Derek Chauvin as a bad actor is too convenient an excuse. Now, am I denying that white people are advantaged by the system? I certainly hope I'm not. But this cannot be narrowly understood in terms of whiteness. This is a system that's extraordinarily complex, and we need to get to those complexities. 'Whiteness' doesn't help us do that. Race is certainly a huge factor in things. But it's part of a larger political economic system and we need to get our heads around the way capitalism and racism are absolutely intertwined with one another, as an integrated justifying system of domination and exploitation.

Part of the problem of laying blame on 'whiteness' is that it cuts off what needs to be a coalitional partnership between oppressed people of all kinds, including white oppressed people. We need to remember the great theorist W. E. B. Du Bois, who said poor white people were given a public and 'psychological wage' that distracted from the fact that they were being exploited, and by the same elites enslaving and indenturing others. The psychological wage told them, 'Well, at least you'd got your white skin going for you.' It was a diversionary tactic, a tactic that introduced a divide-and-conquer strategy between exploited white folks and enslaved Black folks. It's the same thing you saw with the 'Chinese question' during the same time in nineteenth-century America. It's certainly what the great theorist Cedric Robinson found in the UK when he looked at the early histories of industrial exploitation among, say, the Irish and the 'Slavs' in relationship to the English. Robinson saw how race was being deployed to divide *Europeans*. He knew right away that race was not about biology. It wasn't a biological distinction. It was a labour distinction. He realized automatically that race is not about difference. It's about differentiation. Race is not about diversity, or diversification. It's about stratification. These are ploys used to divide us.

So what I think we have to push for is most powerfully articulated in the Trinidadian-American Marxist Oliver Cromwell Cox. What he pointed to is the need to look past the local forms of oppression, and look for coalitional kinds of solidarity – politics across the classes of oppressed people all across the world. These are the ways we begin a revolution, by looking past the fictions meant to oppress and divide us. The picture I'm presenting involves a path to liberation. And it begins with solidarity that cuts across the forms of racial nationalism that tempt us.

What I truly appreciate about the church in San Francisco is their deep dependence on the Black church in San Francisco. They depend on the Black churches there. Everything for them is about how they belong in this place with others. They have always had this sense that if they are going to live there, they're going to have to do so within the gift structure of these relationships. One of the people I interviewed was the pastor of a local Black church. He said that one of the things that is so important about Redeemer, which has many Asian Americans, is that being in Black San Francisco teaches it about Black life. It's this willingness to be present or, as Christians would say, 'incarnate' that enables them to see the sightlines of oppression. What happens when you're only paid this much? What happens when local businesses are crushed? They're able to see those sightlines. And then they're also able to see, with their neighbours, sightlines to liberation. The partnership with these other churches then led to recognizing the need for jobs and education, and it was from that that they eventually created the business and the school. It came from them living with their neighbours and asking how we might create infrastructures that bring justice.

Here's the fundamental difference between all that I've been talking about and the Marxism that runs alongside it. Marxism is waiting for the revolution to start, and inciting radical democratic action in order to ignite it, and this is good work. Christians are not waiting for something to start; they're laying claim to a revolution that's already started, now 2,000 years ago. And if Christians are right about the natural order of things, that justice and mercy are natural to our world because they are natural to God, then we're laying claim to the most natural parts of who we are. Redeemer, for all its extraordinary brilliance and faithfulness, is just doing what all of us can be doing – what HeartEdge is doing right with its emphasis on commerce and local congregations. My sense is this stuff is happening all over the world.

11 March 2021

12

Maggi Dawn

Creativity

'Culture' is one of those malleable words that takes on assorted meanings depending on the context. One way it's commonly used is to refer to literature and the arts, and, used in this sense, 'culture' intersects with many aspects of faith, from theology, to mission, to worship and more. I want to share a few ideas about how we engage broadly with the arts in our liturgy and worship, through poetic language, use of space, music, choreographed movement, visual symbols and ritual actions. The arts are more than merely a way of expressing what we think, or how we feel; they also shape our beliefs and emotions. On the surface of it, for instance, we are aware that we sing songs or use particular prayers or actions to express joy or praise or lament. But over the course of time, more than just giving us a mode of expression, they also shape our beliefs, our feelings and our sense of identity as faith communities. They do so not only through statements that are made but through the intangible messages they deliver. As we sing and pray, stand or sit, in buildings that look a certain way, and have their own smell and sound and atmosphere, all that visual and aural experience builds and shapes our faith, and so it's worth paying careful attention to both the content and the performance of our worship.

In the discussion of the arts, the word 'culture' is sometimes used in a rather pejorative way. Proponents of popular culture can be dismissed as unsophisticated, while someone else might be referred to as 'very cultured' – meaning that they prefer Rossini to Radiohead, or Bach to the Beatles. Yet the idea that high art is more cultured or sophisticated than popular culture is, I believe, a mistake. You can certainly find poor quality work in the pop music business, but equally there is some pretty awful classical music. Kurt Weill, who was renowned for constantly transgressing the boundary between high art and popular culture, was quoted in *The New Republic* as saying, 'I have never acknowledged the difference between "serious" and "light" music. There is only good music and bad music.' But does the assessment of good or bad go beyond accepting multiple genres? Does it also apply to the quality of performance? And if so, does that imply that our expressions of worship are predominantly voiced by professional artists or skilled amateurs? What about the rest of us? Perhaps part of the answer to this is to engage the skilled artists not only in performance but also in enabling the performance of worship by the whole congregation.

One of my formative experiences (which was also great fun!) was my role as Dean of Chapel at Yale Divinity School, where I had the opportunity to work within a community that was both widely ecumenical and artistically highly accomplished. The school encompassed more than 35 different denominations, as well as those who did not claim any denominational allegiance. Once a day, every weekday, all the way through the academic year, we came together for a chapel service. Due to the integration of the Divinity School with the Yale Institute of Sacred Music, Worship and the Arts, our congregation included many practitioners or students of the arts, so we were able to draw on exceptional talent as we wove music and the arts into our worship. But we also explored the idea that the role of an artist in church might include enabling congregational worship. Sometimes highly skilled visual or musical artists would not only perform, but show the congregation what otherwise seemed mysterious about their skills in order to enable new means of expression. Thus the artists were not only performers, but leaders in community worship. The results were often very particular, both to our congregation and to the moment in which they were created. We made some community art that you wouldn't want to hang in a gallery, or keep for ever; and we sang some songs that were right for the moment but certainly not publishable. Now, this work was not shabby; sometimes it really was beautiful. But the point is that it allowed our worship to be expressed through the arts not only by the most talented but by the whole community; and it also meant that we came to understand the arts not only as creations of permanent quality, they could also be ephemeral.

This point about the arts being 'in the moment', and not necessarily for posterity, relates to an idea St Augustine explored. He is sometimes misunderstood as being rather against the arts, whereas he was actually much in favour, but he did point out that the beauty of artistic endeavour can pose a danger to faith and worship. If an artist creates something of stunning beauty, that is good. But its beauty should function in such a way that the viewer sees through the thing itself to perceive the source of beauty beyond itself – which, of course, is God. But the danger is that you can look at a beautiful object and then begin to want to hold on to it for ever, perhaps to own it, and the 'thing-ness' of it becomes an end in itself. While you are taken up with wanting the thing, you fail to see God as the source; or even worse, perhaps you think you've got God when all you've got is the thing.

We explored this idea often at Yale, where I invited a number of visiting artists to work with me at Marquand Chapel. One of these artists, Ted Lyddon Hatton, worked almost entirely in ephemeral art, partly in response to Augustine's idea. Ted wants his work to inspire people, to draw them through beauty into a connection with God. But once that connection has been experienced, he dismantles the work, so that what people are left with is the memory of the connection, rather than the opportunity to own, capture or revisit the work. This also leads Ted to make his work both responsive to the particular situation of the community he is visiting and site-specific to the building.

The art he creates is also designed to reflect and shape the particular experiences and needs of the community in the moment – it's beautiful, but temporary. Whether for a week, or a month or however long, once the time is over, the work is not just moved to another location but completely dismantled, and the 'ingredients' swept up, packed in boxes and sent away. For Ted, this is absolutely deliberate: he wants to leave the community with an experience of encounter, not merely impress them with the beauty of a thing.

Ted often works in a technique he calls 'dry painting'. He uses various granular or powdered substances and then sprinkles and blends them on to a surface – a floor or table – as if they are paint. The first time he came to Yale, as Ted was planning what to bring, he called me on the phone and explained that he wanted to use substances that not only gave him a range of colours, but would also allow symbolic meanings to emerge in the art.

'Tell me a bit about your community,' he said. 'I'm bringing some crushed myrrh, and salt and sugar. But I want to know what I could use that would connect to the community. Tell me where the community gathers – where does that "water cooler" thing happen?'

I said, 'Well, after chapel, every day, we have our "coffee hour" in the common room – it isn't really an hour, it's only about 25 minutes. But that's where we gather. Whatever happened in chapel might spill over into conversation, but also people who don't come to chapel do come to coffee hour, so it's an important part of the day and a lot of our community life springs from it.'

'Okay,' said Ted. 'Here's an idea – between now and when I come to visit, can you save the coffee grounds after you've had coffee hour, and dry them?'

I volunteered that we could just as easily buy him fresh coffee.

'No,' he said, 'I don't want fresh coffee. I want the grounds that are left over from the coffee you actually drank.'

Drying used coffee grounds took some effort. We spread them out thinly on a long table at the back of chapel, turning them daily until they were thoroughly dry and didn't go mouldy. A sign on the table said, 'Why are we drying used coffee? Watch this space ...' That built a sense of curiosity and anticipation among the community. By the time Ted arrived a couple of months later, we had several buckets full of dried coffee ready for use.

The very first day he arrived, I gathered a group of students to meet Ted, and after a few introductions and some general chitchat, he grabbed a handful of the dried coffee from one of the buckets, and said, 'Tell me about your coffee hour, and your conversations. Why is this so essential to your community?' One by one, the students volunteered that they needed the caffeine to get through the next lecture, or they depended on having a half-hour of social time to break the silence of so many hours in the library. One said that it was the place he was guaranteed to meet his friends, and another mentioned that the professors also come to coffee hour, and it's one of the few chances she got to talk to them outside class.

I'll never forget what happened next. One person had said nothing so far, but as the table went quiet, he spoke up. 'I know this might sound harsh,' he said, 'because all those good things are true. But I think we should admit that the brand of coffee we drink tastes quite bitter, and, to be completely honest, sometimes our conversations are rather bitter as well.' The whole table went quiet. Someone had said out loud what nobody else had dared to say. And then people began to admit that, yes, there were aspects to our community life that were painful and difficult. The conversations were often sweet, but sometimes they were bitter.

The disjunction between sweetness and the bitterness became a central feature of everything that followed that week in chapel. Ted gave everyone a few grains of the crushed myrrh he had brought with him, explaining that because most people remember it as the substance that was brought to the burial of Jesus, it's often associated with death and grief. But he explained that myrrh is a resin produced by the dindin tree whenever its bark is cut or wounded. The resin pours out of the cut to heal the tree, and then dries into the hard substance that is harvested and crushed for use as incense. 'So,' said Ted, 'myrrh is not ultimately about death and dying, but about healing and new life. And wherever there is bitterness, brokenness, we need this healing.

Ted proceeded to create enormous floor paintings in the chapel, using the myrrh, some liquefaction (the silky, sandy and sinister substance that emerges from an earthquake) and various other powders and grains, and the coffee that represented a certain bitterness, and throughout the week we considered themes of brokenness and healing. At the end of the week, in our final service of the week, Ted told the congregation he wanted them to help him to sweep up the paintings, and for a moment people sat glued to their seats – how could we possibly destroy this beautiful work? But first, he gave everybody a tiny, empty bottle with a cork in the top, and invited everyone to scoop up a few grains of myrrh. Then he told us all to go out all across the Yale campus, and wherever there was a need for healing, to sprinkle a few grains of myrrh as an act of healing prayer. For weeks afterwards people talked about Ted's visit – but not just about the art. The art was beautiful, and we had some photos to remind us of it, but nobody could buy it and take it home. Instead, we were left with the impact it had on us as a community, and the ongoing awareness that we could carry the intent for beauty, and prayer, and healing, and mending relationships, wherever we went. And as well as being ephemeral, it was very particular to our community. If he'd come to St Martin-in-the-Fields, he'd have found out what was happening in your community and made something quite different.

What we experienced with Ted Lyddon Hatton was not something you can produce every day – it was a special event in our year, with more time and energy and budget devoted to it than normal. Not every liturgy can be that experimental or unusual, or demand that level of investment. Nevertheless, I believe there is something valuable in learning to approach even our 'everyday' liturgies with the attitude of an artist. Why? Because when people get together to plan an event, both the processes and the results are quite different if you operate with a creative model rather than a business meeting model. When I was in my teens and considering what to do with my life, it was unclear to me whether I should be an artist or a musician, because I was equally good at both. I was lucky enough to have fantastic teachers who not only taught me technique but pushed me to imagine what I might want to do that was not quite like anything I'd seen already. I began making sculptures from found objects, which was not on the syllabus, but which I've continued to do ever since. And in addition to the hours of practice you spend in the music room mastering the classics, I was encouraged to write my own music, again not writing like everyone else did, but re-imagining sounds I knew into new formations. From those formative years, what I've carried with me into the practice of liturgy is that training I accrued in thinking like a creative. And one of the ways I've trained my liturgical teams over the course of several decades is to move away from the model of 'worship planning' that operates like a committee or a business meeting. Instead, we have worked on a creative model, letting one idea spark another until eventually something quite fresh and original emerges. Only then do we return to budgets and logistics and all the things necessary to bring the idea into reality.

Creativity is not only about bringing new things into old structures. It's also about understanding the impact of elements in liturgical experience that are often taken for granted. Too often the construction of a service is done on a screen or on paper, at a desk, focusing almost entirely on the words on the page; what those words say, what they mean, and who says them. But just as a play is made up of more than its script, a liturgy is more than the words on the page – it's all the movements, sounds, ritual action, and music, which may be noted but are not enacted on the page, and beyond that it's also the way the light plays in the building, the acoustic quality, the proximity of seating, and whether the choir is visible to the congregation or divided by a screen. Every part of the liturgy as it is enacted affects the experience, and consequently a service in two neighbouring churches could, in theory, look identical on the page and yet be dramatically different.

What is your setting like? Is it an enormous, imposing space that delivers a sense of transcendence, or a small and intimate venue with almost the feeling of a sitting room? Is it a physical space, an online space, or a hybrid? What does it look like – light and airy, or dark and rich? And what does it smell like – 150 years of incense and prayers, or the lingering smell of coffee and company? All those things affect what happens liturgically. One is not better or worse than the other, they are just different, and to tune in to your particular space is to ask what that particular space invites and makes possible.

I mentioned online and hybrid spaces just now. Liturgy and worship happen when people come together in time and space, but something that the recent experience of lockdown has made everyone far more aware of is that the time we meet may be concurrent, or recorded, or across time zones. And the space may be physical or digital. The time and space in which we find ourselves affects the experience of connectedness we have – to God, to ideas and to one another. So it's important to understand those features.

For instance, the building we meet in will affect us by its size, light, lines of sight, acoustic, smell, and so on, but if the meeting is in hybrid form, how does the experience vary between those who are in the building physically or digitally? Since the first lockdown, I think I've only been in a church building once in 14 months. At first, I think people commonly thought that online worship was a temporary replacement for being in the building. If there have been any good things to come out of the pandemic, perhaps it is the much wider recognition that online space is actually a place. I'm not pretending to be at St Martin-in-the-Fields for this talk;

I'm in my study in Durham. But I'm not disembodied. I'm situated in time and place – and so are you. So there's a sense in which the internet creates a different kind of place. What is this hybrid space like? How can we get comfortable in it, and nestle in a bit? It sounds and looks different from the place we are familiar with, but it is a place nonetheless – and I think this experience will be important to hold on to when we once again have the freedom to meet in physical spaces without restrictions. I think the worst thing we could do is to try to return to exactly what we did before – if we do that, we will lose something valuable. It bears saying that there are people who have known this for a long time – for instance, some who cannot get to the building because of illness, or for other physical reasons.

One of the notable things about church being pushed into online space is the way communities have expanded across the globe. Wherever I am in any corner of the church or world, I might get invited to speak somewhere far away. In the last few months I've spoken in Auckland, New York, London and Edinburgh, without even leaving my own study. And I hope we don't lose that. Communities are not just local: they're not just in the middle of London or Auckland or New York. I check in at the cathedral down the road from me for morning prayer most mornings – even though it's less than a mile away, there have been months when I could only go there online. But the community has not diminished, it has grown. Prior to lockdown, you'd find a dozen or so people at morning prayer on any given day, almost all of whom live very locally. But since the service went online, I've found myself praying with more than a hundred people from all around the world – not only attending to the Daily Office (the order of service), but also making personal connections in the chat facility, and promising to pray personally for one another. It would be really sad if we lost that when our buildings open up again; if we can continue to think in terms of expanded space, that would be really a good thing.

All this talk of the arts is all very well, but you might be thinking that not everyone is good at the arts. Is what I've been describing just a very niche approach for artsy people? I think it's more than that – and it's also worth saying, first, that excellent engagement in the arts will speak to people whether they are 'into' that in a particular way or not, and, second, that to do any of this well you need other skills too – people who are skilled in organization, and logistical matters, and health and safety, and all kinds of things. You need people who can organize things, who can hang stuff up, make things work, draw in the congregation, make the coffee for afterwards. One year at Yale, I had a marvellous team member called Kevin. When he applied to join the chapel team, he told me, 'I don't really do the arts at all, but I like what you do, and I'd really like to work on your team to learn more.' We talked a while, and it was clear he had plenty to offer, as well as an enormous desire to learn. Some months later, we were putting together a huge, sculpted arrangement that had been designed by one of the trained designers on the team, and to make this installation work we needed to hang a set of ropes from the ceiling. The design was clear as to how it needed to hang, but we were puzzling over exactly how to get all the pieces in the right place. Then Kevin stood up, pointed at the team members one by one, and said, 'You stand there, you move that way, you pick up this rope, you hold this over your head, now everyone pull on the piece of rope you are holding.' Bit by bit he organized everyone in the room, and within a couple of hours the whole arrangement went up. Afterwards I asked him, 'How did you figure that out?' 'Oh, well,' he replied, 'there was something I didn't tell you before, but I used to be an engineer. I don't know how to design things, but I know how to make designs work!' We need all kinds of skills. For every artist, we also need an engineer, administrator, events manager, accountant, lawyer, health and safety expert ... and so on! To inject our liturgical life with a fresh layer of art and design needs more than poets and painters – it needs a host of skills.

Sometimes people ask me to show them how to 'use the arts' to promote the gospel, or to liven up their worship. I understand the intent, but I think the idea that you can 'use' the arts to add a bit of glitz to what's already there is a fundamental misunderstanding of how the arts function. The arts are hopelessly limited if we assume that we already have the message, and we just need the arts to dress things up and make them more attractive. Going back to what I said about the creative process, again there is that difference between starting out with an outcome already in mind, or allowing for creativity and letting go of the controls. You're not really allowing for creativity or imagination if you already know what the outcome is. (The same is even true for science, or any kind of research or development – there may be an intent and a direction, but any kind of exploration has to begin with the assumption that there is something out there we don't yet know, or haven't yet seen or thought of.) For the church to engage fully in the arts requires a degree of relinquishment of control, because the arts can only speak if you let them have their own voice. To write a sermon and then go and look for a painting or a poem that proves the point is to silence the arts, not to let them speak.

There's an anecdote about Robert Schumann playing piano at a salon concert, when he introduced his latest composition to the audience. After much applause, one member of the audience asked him, 'Mr Schumann, that was beautiful, but can you tell us what it means?' After a pause, and without a word, he sat down at the piano and played it again. The story illustrates the fact that 'What does music mean?' is one of the most elusive questions. It is endlessly debated by musicologists who try to identify exactly why this or that piece of music evokes certain feelings. Why does a minor key sound mournful in some cultures, but makes others want to get up and dance? Why does speeding up or slowing down a piece of music by just one or two beats per minute change its sense so dramatically? I did some research on why people in churches use a certain repertoire for their hymns and songs, whether that's pop songs or traditional hymns. I asked people who were organists and choral directors, or who led guitar bands in worship. The first question I asked was, 'How do you choose the music for any given Sunday?', and far and away the most predominant answer was that they chose according to lyrical content. They would look up the readings for the day, or the theme the preacher was going to address, or the season being celebrated, such as Ascension, or Easter, and then go and find hymns and songs with lyrics that reflected the theme. But later I asked them, 'When you've introduced a hymn or song, and seen the response in your congregation, how do you decide whether you will use it again?' Almost every person replied that they judged by congregational response – whether they were singing along, whether the expressions on their faces and their body language showed real engagement, whether the volume of singing went up, and whether they picked up the tune easily and accurately. 'Everyone could sing it, just like that,' said one music leader, 'we'll definitely sing that again.' And another said, 'This song was full of hope, it just makes you want to process out of church and back into the world.' What was interesting about this is that the music leaders were judging the effectiveness of a song mostly according to musical considerations, yet still they continued to choose hymns according to lyrical content. Instead, why don't we ask ourselves how the whole song – the music and the lyrics together – create both an atmosphere and expression of worship, and leave a sensibility of theological meaning that is not delivered by words alone? Supposing, for instance, on Easter morning, you want to capture the sense that a secret is about to be revealed, a surprise that will change the world, something remarkable that only begins today but continues to unfold gradually over the next 50 days of Easter and beyond. What music will create a sense of anticipation and mystery, before the world explodes into joy? We say the words 'He is risen', but their meaning will sink into our hearts if they are voiced in music and action and the use of space, so that we quite viscerally create the sense that the world is about to open up in new ways. To allow the arts to do their work, you have to let them speak in their own voice. Let the building tell its story; let the music do the talking.

I've talked a bit about how to get creative processes and thinking into the way we plan and design our liturgical life. Let me tell you about one instance of this. Most churches have a few huge and special occasions every year, such as Easter or Christmas. Unlike weekly services that typically repeat a similar format with variations, these big festivals often involve special music, extra decorations, and more planning and rehearsal than usual. In university chapels, Christmas and Easter are when people go away, and so it was that, when I worked at Yale, we held our biggest service of the year just before the semester ended for the winter break. The Advent Service was different every year, each one a huge creative production, and in the weeks beforehand anticipation would build as the community waited to see what it would be like this time.

To create the Advent Service, weeks beforehand I would gather my team in a room with a huge table, roll out a huge piece of old wallpaper on a table, and put pens and paint and markers all around the room. The team was as widely ecumenical as the congregation. Some of them knew so much about Advent they simply took it for granted, and for others it was a complete novelty. I used to come with half a dozen 'starter' ideas. I threw out some classic Advent thoughts such as darkness and light, or waiting for the unexpected, or Nativity and Maranatha. I took along some lines from a poem, or an image or two, or a piece of music. Having put all these ideas out on the table, I would ask, 'What does that make you think of?' And the team would start brainstorming. The only rule of the meeting was that no one was allowed to say, 'We can't afford it', or, 'That's a stupid idea', or, 'We don't have the resources', or, 'We couldn't do that, it's too complicated.' The rule of the meeting was, you can't say no, you can only say, 'That makes me think of ...'; you can add, but you can't take away. We walked around this table for a couple of hours, talking, dreaming, asking questions, saying, 'Say more about that ...', and filling the paper with doodles and images and words. I always appointed a couple of people whose role was specifically to write notes as other people were talking. And we ended up with a roll of wallpaper covered in ideas.

I would then take the paper away and hang it on my study wall, and over the next four or five days I would stand and look at this wall of words and shapes and things. Gradually, no matter how random the connections seemed to be, or how messy or complicated it looked, something would begin to emerge from it. The aim was never to choose one idea that was better than the rest. And it was never a majority vote thing – to choose pilgrimage, or stars, or darkness and light, because that got more references than anything else. It was much more organic than that. Something none of us had thought of, something no one had clearly articulated, would rise out of that mess of ideas. And I would then frame that idea, put it back to the team. What amazed me was the consistency with which the team would say, 'Yes! That's it! That is what we were reaching for!' And then they followed on with more focused ideas to encapsulate what we wanted to do.

This process is not neat planning, but neither is it spontaneity. We never said we would just improvise (although, by the way, in the world of the arts, improvisation isn't quite the same thing as spontaneity – it only occurs after hundreds of hours of rehearsal!). Rather, we were allowing the creative process to enable us to find something that we hadn't thought of before, but once we had thought of it, then we imagined it into being. And yes, in some ways it might be a little risky, although I would say, in terms of opening ourselves up to truth and revelation, that it's just as risky to nail everything down neatly and leave no room for the imagination.

This is a very Coleridgean thought. Samuel Coleridge said the one thing that really sets the human race apart as made in the image of God is that we're able to create something out of nothing – we can imagine a world into being, and then make it happen. And I think that, as we emerge from the pandemic, and look forward into a future that will undoubtedly throw a whole new set of uncertainties our way, we shouldn't assume we can go back to what we did before, but neither should we just let the future come at us and see what happens. Rather, we could draw on our creative faculties, to take what we knew and loved before lockdown disrupted our lives; then to look at what we learned during lockdown and identify what was not just a temporary fix, but a discovery of new and untried ways of worship. We could allow those ideas to interact with what we've heard happens elsewhere, or things we have imagined but never yet tried. We could lay all those ideas out side by side, mix them up, let them speak, and see what emerges. We might imagine modes of worship that are dramatically different, or that are just a sideways take on what we have done before. But, having imagined it, we could try it out and see if it works. We don't have to go back to normal, and we don't have to plan or legislate our worship in committees and business meetings. Instead, we can create it by playing like an artist.

8 April 2021

13

Stephen Cottrell

Faithfulness

Lent has felt very long this year. One long experience of having one's life stripped back. And although I don't underestimate how incredibly hard it's been, nor the awful suffering that many people have experienced and are experiencing across our world, I must acknowledge that there has also been something refining about the experience of lockdown and pandemic – putting us back in touch with our own mortality and frailty, and experiencing the Christian life without all the familiar comforts, even the sacraments themselves. It has been like a long Lent. Like a desert. And in Christian spirituality, the desert is always a place of encounter.

When I stopped being Bishop of Chelmsford on Easter Day last year, two or three weeks into the first lockdown, knowing my love of the Scottish painter Craigie Aitchison, Chelmsford Diocese bought me a print of his that has hung in my study ever since. I've spent a lot of time looking at it in the past year. For those of you who know his paintings, it is a familiar image. He painted just about the same picture over and over again: Christ is on the cross; the background is a Rothko-esque landscape of vivid colour; and usually a dog sits patiently at the foot of the cross.

Because the experience of lockdown has been a stripping away of faith until all I have left is Christ, this image of a very isolated Christ has spoken into my own isolation. For we've been living without much else. We're not allowed to touch each other. We're not allowed to embrace. We can't meet. We can't go to church. We don't receive the sacraments. We don't have the fellowship we long for. Yet Christ remains. And with him in Aitchison's passion narratives, one other creature – a faithful dog.

When I first saw one of these paintings – and there are hundreds of them – I remember looking at it and thinking, 'Even dogs come to the cross!' But the more I looked, I found myself saying, 'Only dogs come to the cross.' Something about the faithful obedience of the dog seated at the foot of the cross spoke to me powerfully about the waiting and watching I am called to, and where I need to sit. Craigie Aitchison's pictures also pick up strong environmental themes. He sometimes paints pictures without Christ, but he rarely paints a picture without a dog.

Abba Moses, one of the Desert Fathers, told his novices, 'Go to your cell: your cell will teach you everything.' Desperate though it's been at times, the experience of the past year has been, for me, one of simply trying to be with Christ – and with everything else stripped back. It's been a painful, though not unrewarding, education in the spiritual life.

Every ten years, stipendiary clergy in the Church of England have the great gift of a sabbatical. Four years ago, on my sabbatical, I walked to Santiago de Compostela. I opted for the northern route, mainly because I knew that very few people walked that way. You're not accompanied by crowds of pilgrims – and as well as craving the road, I was craving some solitude. Again, it was an experience of isolation, walking day after day on my own – a refining Lenten experience.

One of the things it gave me was a new love of the Lord's Prayer. I keep coming back to the petition, 'Give us today our daily bread.' I have, of course, said this prayer a lot. And although I wasn't brought up in the church, I've said it every day for the last 45 years. But it's only recently that I've really started wondering what it means. Especially that petition which accompanied me across northern Spain: give me today enough for today; stop me, prevent me, hold me back from wanting more than my share. I'm therefore caught between, on the one hand, the incredible biblical theme of abundance, God's astonishing profusion – everyone's fed and there's 12 baskets left over; an inebriated group of wedding guests are given the one thing they don't need, more alcohol – but on the other hand, challenged to learn to live with enough, and to learn what enough looks like.

It's hard to imagine a more important question for the whole world to wrestle with at the moment: what is enough? The wisdom in the Christian tradition about the relationship between feasting and fasting might help us to develop not just a theology but a way of living, which is both sustainable – learning what enough looks like, asking for no more than my daily bread – and at the same time not losing the great gift of abundance, the festival and feast. There are many movements in the church, and even more in the world, looking at how we slow down. The church could take a lead. It is something the isolation is teaching us. We need to recover lost disciplines, like making and mending, like recycling. Second-hand is now often referred to as pre-loved. I laughed when I first heard this. However, I don't laugh any more, because that's what we have to recover.

What I see in Jesus Christ is that pattern of feast and fast – the ability to enter deeply into the joy of life and the festival of life and the feast of life, while also acknowledging the beauty and power of the widow's mite and seeking out isolation and solitude. I am both overwhelmed by God – God is far too much – and at the same time empty and hungry for more.

Though I also acknowledge that I'm just a beginner in the spiritual life, and would hate it if anyone listening to me thought that I've got it all worked out (I can absolutely assure you I haven't). That's one of the reasons I keep coming back to the Lord's Prayer. I think it might have been Thérèse of Lisieux, whom I love, who said, 'If you could say the Lord's Prayer once and truly mean it, you would be in heaven.' The fact that I'm still saying it is ample evidence that this is not yet true for me, that I still have much to learn and much to relinquish, that I still haven't learned how to say it and truly mean it.

Texts like the Lord's Prayer, the Ten Commandments, the Beatitudes, the creeds have always been central to the catechetical work of the church. We've lost that a bit – that to learn to be a Christian is to learn to say the Lord's Prayer; to learn the ethical life that God has given us in the Ten Commandments; to live out the Beatitudes. In previous generations, as you were schooled in the Christian life, so you received, imbibed and lived out these texts. They shaped you. In the work I'm involved in with the church nationally, one of my hopes is that there will be a renewal of formation and catechesis. And with it, a greater theological literacy. Not so that we can all have a degree in God, but so that we can be formed in the Christian life. Because it's a good life.

It would be unusual to find anyone whose mental health has not suffered in the last year. I know mine has. I've watched more TV than in most of the rest of my life put together. (I watched *Breaking Bad* for the first time. My kids have been telling me to watch that for years. I got round to it in 2020 and thoroughly enjoyed it.)

Mental health, physical health, emotional health and spiritual health are tied up with one another. We human beings are a totality. The greatest danger is when we start compartmentalizing these things, or worse, construct a kind of hierarchy: that one kind of illness is somehow worse or more serious than another. I try to hold on to the Christian vision of what it is to be human, and certainly do not see mental health as being any less or more difficult for faith than any other sorts of health. But I do know the stigmas attached to it mean that some people of faith feel that mental illness is something they should hide. It touches on the Christian ministry of healing. Perhaps that's really where we need to do a bit more work.

It has indeed been a very long Lent. I still feel as if I'm longing to sing Alleluia because it's not meant to be Lent all the time. And since I am a Christian whose life is shaped and sustained by the church and its liturgical and sacramental life, it is very hard to live the Christian life without those things. A piece of scripture that I've found really helpful in the past year has been the story of the woman who was suffering for many years from haemorrhages. Out of her grace and goodness, she doesn't touch Jesus because, if she touched him, she would make him unclean. She touches just the hem of his garment, but she receives his complete presence. I found this story incredibly helpful in my isolation, for although I cannot receive the sacraments, nor participate in the life of the church in the ways that usually sustain me, Jesus is not absent. I have been touching the hem of his garment. Though I still look forward to the embrace, which is beginning to re-emerge.

If ours is a sacramental faith, those sacraments are not optional extras. They're there for a reason – and the reason is that we human beings are this totality of mind, body, spirit, emotions and all the rest of it. The classic Anglican definition holds good: these are outward and visible signs of inward and spiritual grace. And we need them. I worry for our church when we downgrade and undervalue the sacraments and see them as somehow optional to the Christian life. They are absolutely central – until that day when we see him face to face. That's why I'm not one of those clergy who wants to be buried in my vestments. Sacraments are for this life. The scriptures tell us that in that city 'there is no temple' (Revelation 21.23).

There have been many failures of the church. I don't know whether I can speak much wisdom into that, but I will, and I am trying to. What is needed is humility and honesty. But what's also needed is action. We have to become a different church; one which is less defended, less lawyered up, more able to invite, especially those who have been most hurt by the church – to invite them into the room so they might help us be the church we need to become. I'm trying to be a voice for that. I'm trying to speak regularly with people who have been survivors and victims of abuse in the church. We can learn from their experience. All of us carry damage, and it's very rare to find somebody who hasn't been damaged in some way by what's hit them in life. I'm deeply embarrassed and ashamed of the church's failings and I've seen the consequences of it first-hand. Often, in the past, our response has been not just inadequate: it's added further abuse. That must change – and I believe is changing.

I want us to be a church that looks like Jesus. What I see in Jesus is astonishing compassion for those who have been damaged in life. But I also see righteousness: a longing for justice and reconciliation. That's what you might call the second mile, the distance that we still have to go. What, after all, is peace? Peace could be the silence after the guns have finished firing. Or it could be reconciliation painfully embraced. It's that second vision of peace that I long for.

There's no point in pretending we're in a good place on some of these issues. We could add others, such as racial injustice and racism in the church. There are things we need to do; silence isn't a proper response, though a waiting upon God and a penitent spirit are certainly needed. We have to rise up and act and help the church to act differently. We need to demonstrate a different way of being a more Christ-centred and more Jesus-shaped church. In some ways this is such an obvious thing to say: we should be more like followers of Jesus. But we also know it is the most profound. And the work of a lifetime. That's what I'm working towards. It's something I speak about a lot. You don't get to be a bishop if you're not reasonably good at talking, but when it comes to a Christ-like life, it's not the words that matter, it's not just about talking a good game. It is about the lives we lead. Lent is always a time for resetting the compass of our discipleship. This long Lent has helped us see that what matters is our rootedness in Christ and how that shapes who we are.

We therefore also need to speak about sin and the ways we fall short and how we face up to this through repentance. This is always the first step in the renewal of our life in Christ. Then we need to rise up. If we don't, we commit the sin of idolatry, which is close to the heart of most sins. We create and worship something other than God.

When I go to North America, I'm usually greeted by people who say to me, 'Gee, I love your accent.' The typical kind of Brit response is, 'No, I don't have an accent. I speak normally. You're the one who has the accent.' Now, just in that trivial example, what I've demonstrated is that I consider myself to be the centre. I am normal. Everything else outside of me is therefore abnormal, not quite normal enough, less than normal. That is the beginning of an idolatrous view of self, which the Christian faith comes to redeem and reconfigure, showing us that we have a new humanity in Christ, where there is no Jew or Gentile, there is no slave nor free, there is no man and woman, but a new humanity. In the great vision at the end of the book of Revelation every tribe, every tongue, every people, every nation is gathered together. It is the fulfilment of the mission that begins at Pentecost. However, if I'd been in charge at Pentecost – if you can forgive such a thought! – I would have done things differently. I would have got the whole world to speak the same language – a kind of holy Esperanto would have been a much better way of launching a world mission. The Holy Spirit does the precise opposite: not the world speaking one language, but the church speaking every language. Diversity is embraced and celebrated. Moreover, the biblical narrative confronts the idolatrous human narrative. Consequently, I'm not ashamed or embarrassed to talk about sin and repentance. Repentance means reorientation, a complete change in the way we shape and direct our lives – what you might call the absolute necessity of being eccentric. And to have your centre outside yourself begins with the dethroning of self.

To borrow a phrase from the Archbishop of Canterbury, I long for us to improve the quality of our disagreements. To achieve this would be a good thing, but I long for more. If you look, for instance, at the continuing process regarding the place of ordained women in the church, the key breakthrough happened 30 or 40 years ago, when a Lambeth Conference passed a resolution that said something like, 'Whether you agree with or dissent from the ordination of women to the priesthood and the episcopate, you are a loyal Anglican.' Once that was agreed, everything else was just a matter of time. The Rubicon has been crossed. We've acknowledged that it's okay to disagree. Everything else follows.

With regard to the debates and disagreement around issues in human sexuality, I would love us to get to a similar point where we are able to acknowledge the boundaries of appropriate and respectful disagreement. I believe Living in Love and Faith (LLF) may get us to that point. There are other things I'd love to see beyond that, and I don't know when or how that will happen. But for me, the biblical vision is of the new humanity we have in Christ, which embraces and reconfigures our diversity, recognizing that, in that diversity, we are all made in the image of God. We need to work out what that means, and how we live it out, especially with our disagreements. I'm not going to say I'm optimistic, but I'm deeply hopeful. Why? Because the Christian narrative demands it. This is not, therefore, about identity politics or culture wars. It is the outworking of the revelation of God in Jesus Christ.

It grieves me that people who are living in stable faithful relationships feel excluded from the church. But there's still a piece of theological work that needs to be done, and I am hopeful that LLF will deliver that, and change the narrative so that it's no longer about one side winning over another, but everyone agreeing that these are areas where it's possible to disagree, and then finding ways to live with our disagreement with integrity. I don't think that's a fudge. I know some people may think it is. One of the things people find hardest is that for some people, that's an opinion, whereas for other people, it's their whole life and identity. I completely get that, and I'm frustrated that we are where we are.

Throughout my life, what has motivated me is peacemaking, reconciliation and concern for our poorest communities. At one of the great councils of the church in Galatians, Paul with his wisdom and intellect and rhetoric wins the day. And just at the end, Peter says to him, 'Remember the poor.' 'Well, of course,' Paul says, 'that's what I always intended.' But the church frequently forgets the poor. Working for peace, remembering the poor, and trying to build a world that works for peace and remembers the poor – that's our mission.

When people ask me, what's your favourite story in the Bible, I say the story of Shadrach, Meshach and Abednego. When they're about to be put into the burning fiery furnace, because they refuse to worship Nebuchadnezzar's golden statue, they say, 'We believe that our God can save us. But even if he doesn't, we're not going to serve your gods to worship a statue' (see Daniel 3.1–18). I love that. Doesn't that define faithfulness? I don't care if people keep on telling me how naive I am. Or keep on saying that it's foolish to think that the church could live together with disagreement. I'm going to carry on saying it – because it's what I see in Christ. I keep coming back to that statement: we're not going to worship that statue of yours. It doesn't matter. You can throw us in the fire. We're just not going to do it.

Another way of understanding what's happened in the last year, beyond Lent and fasting, is exile – which is where that story comes from. In exile, Israel discovered who they were. If I think about what the church has discovered in this exile, the most obvious thing is that it's been a digital coming of age. Online church is here to stay. And we shouldn't be frightened of that. It doesn't mean we won't be meeting physically as well – of course we will. This might also be one of the ways we save the planet, because the whole planet has breathed a sigh of relief. And as we've stopped charging all over the place and enabled ourselves to watch a bit more telly, we've discovered that there are positives to living this way. Now we urgently need to integrate those lessons into the world we inhabit as we come out of the immediate horrors of the pandemic. Learning how to do community and church and other things online, learning that hybrid life, is going to be a huge part of the future.

If there had been a central diktat from the Church of England (not that the Church of England has this authority anyway), saying, 'We want the whole of the Church of England's worship to move online tomorrow', you can imagine the ridicule that would have been met with. Yet that is what happened. It is simply astonishing. In virtually every church, and some in the most creative ways, churches moved their worship online, did the most amazing things, and built new communities of faith. We don't know where this is going to lead. But it's a nice problem to have. I often tell the clergy I serve to put their problems into two piles. One is labelled 'nice problems'. This is one of them. The nice, and very unexpected, problem – that we've got so many people coming to our online church that we don't quite know what to do with them when the pandemic ends. We should not underestimate the fact that this has arisen because of the creativity, flexibility and adaptability of clergy and lay leaders.

The big question facing the human race is how to inhabit the planet in a sustainable way. Enquiries into the origins of the pandemic point us towards the possibility that the pandemic arose in ways that are connected with our abuse of the planet and spread very quickly because of the ways we inhabit the earth. So, though I'm not saying that God sent the pandemic, we cannot simply say the pandemic came out of nowhere. It came out of a somewhere, which is connected with the way we inhabit the world, and our challenge now is to reflect on that.

I have another favourite passage from scripture: John 6. After the 5,000 being fed, Jesus says to the disciples, 'Gather up the fragments, let nothing be lost.' I believe God is always working to gather up fragments. In the pandemic, I see God inviting us to reflect deeply upon the way we inhabit the planet. I hope and pray that, out of it, we can then begin to tackle the much greater crisis and challenge of the environment in a visionary and more far-reaching way. That's where I see God at work in this, teaching us how to follow Jesus and to live lightly on the earth in this long, long Lent.

13 May 2021

14

Lucy Winkett

Mercy

With reference to church life in particular, I think that improvising is a good way of interpreting what happened during the pandemic. I like jazz and blues, music born of great suffering but which somehow finds a way through. As in 12-bar blues, there have been regular chord changes that have remained throughout the pandemic from before and will continue. The regular pattern of worship, prayer at the centre of our life as a gathered community, repeats and remains. On top of that we have been improvising intensively, making it up as we've gone along. Some of that's been to do with the places our church communities are in: city centres have had a particularly acute time of it in the pandemic. But some of it has been because we've tried really hard from the first moment to go towards it rather than retreat from it.

I think probably for every parish priest there was a good deal of confusion to start with – to get the message that you must shut your church, and public worship is suspended, and then a bit later on you can't go into your church. I never thought I would be asked (ordered!) to do that. How do you celebrate the Eucharist when there's no one there in person? Everything felt, very quickly, very chaotic. It seemed to me my role, which was both a blessing and a cost, was to be utterly present for people as much as possible, and faithful to regular prayer: inhabit the regular chord changes that were recognizable and that remained. If our role as priests is to be a signpost pointing away from ourselves, as far as we can, to a greater reality and a deeper truth, then I felt that my main job, in that first period, was to listen hard, to see if I could hear where those chord changes came, while everything else seemed like it was very confusing, and very chaotic. In some ways, it was quite frightening.

It made me think about time in a different way. Time seemed both to collapse and to contract, so everything was happening at once. One of my favourite concepts is that time is God's gift to us to stop everything happening at once. Time therefore is a merciful gift from God, because it lets us experience life in a way we can cope with. So in a situation where it seemed that everything was coming at you at the same time, one of the things that helped me personally was to be absolutely there (on YouTube) at midday, once a day, in a rhythmic and faithful way. I didn't find that difficult at all, perhaps because it was feeding something that I needed – a rhythm. My instinct as a priest was to be as present as possible and full of as much reassurance as I could possibly be. One of the things I've noticed about leadership in this season is that because no one has known what is going on, and no one has had the map or the answers, the quality that has been needed most has been mercy – forgiveness. I've needed a lot of forgiveness when I've made mistakes, and trust. So if you as a priest or a leader hadn't been able to cultivate a culture that prized mercy and trust before, then you really needed to do it in this chaotic situation.

Something that's exercised me a lot has been, 'What has kept us together?' In the church I serve currently, we are a gathered community. We're not a local community. We haven't been seeing each other on our daily exercise. We have only seen each other on Zoom. We couldn't encourage people to travel to the city centre. It would have been the wrong thing to do. Quite fundamental questions arose quickly: how do you celebrate the Eucharist, which is all about connection and the physicality of eating and drinking together?

At the heart of the Eucharist is the merciful action and nature of God, and the trust that is cultivated by sharing food and drink in an equitable way. I've had to rest on those two elements a lot – mercy and trust – and try to understand what they mean in a new way. I feel I've grown painfully and fast over the past year. I don't think I've learned this much this fast since I was 12, when I was trying to get to grips with maths or French, or whatever it was at school. That exponential pace of learning has been very challenging, exhilarating, and also painful.

Trust in God has been difficult. I'm not usually a person who asks God why things happen. I'm not a railer. I question God a lot, I challenge God; but the theodicy question, the suffering question, hasn't often appeared as part of my spiritual life, even when I have suffered tragedy or loss. But in this situation, I found myself asking: if the movement of the Spirit in Genesis is to bring order out of chaos, then where is that movement of the Spirit, when all seems very chaotic for a really long time? I didn't like all the war analogies that were quite prevalent in the pandemic. I felt it was much more about dismantling of communities. In a really tough situation my instinct, since I play the piano, is to get everyone together, get some beer and, on some level, sing our way through it all. And that was precisely the thing you couldn't do in this situation. The war stuff didn't make any sense to me, because in a war you would get together. And in this situation the only thing that was saving us was keeping ourselves apart from each other. So trust becomes incredibly important, and very difficult to maintain. Zoom is not a format that handles disagreement or conflict very well. Ordinarily in person, in trying to discern the way forward, you'd be able to communicate in ways other than with words, with your body, with silences, with your capacity to exchange with each other. That's much more difficult online. So trust is very easily eroded in those rather metallic, boxy ways of communicating, for all the brilliance of it. That's been very difficult. So trust in God, tricky; trusting each other, very tricky. Trust in leadership has been hard because it's patent that leaders don't know any more than the rest of us. I think that for anyone who's fulfilling a representative role for a community, like a priest or a teacher or an elected person, it's been tough. Not as tough as for key workers on the front line obviously, but tough in a different way.

It's not an accident that in the psalms, mercy and truth are met together. What happened in the pandemic was that a lot of very uncomfortable truth was revealed. The injustices and inequalities of our society were ruthlessly exposed. When truth is told, mercy is needed. That's true about myself before God: whenever the truth is told about me, or whenever I try to tell the truth, mercy is necessary. We've been in a very bracing, truth-telling moment, as a society. Which is a good thing, clearly. Not least the inequitable access to green space, or space at all, inequalities in education and access to healthcare and much more. But alongside that has to come a measure of mercy. We have to try to be both truthful and merciful as a society, or to develop a culture that is itself merciful. That's something I've found myself thinking about. Human beings get it wrong, time and time and time again. That's the whole point. That's why mercy is needed. Because the truth is that human beings will continue to get it wrong and find ways to start again.

All of us clergy have had to find ways to preach our way through the pandemic too. I've always been rather compelled by the apocalyptic themes of Advent – death, judgement, heaven and hell. I remember thinking that these themes have been evident in the pandemic: death has been stalking our land, either personally or by extension; judgement has been harsh; for some, the peace of some areas has been a sign of heaven – the air has been cleaner, the birds have been audible, the planes have stopped flying, so there are some people for whom this hiatus has been an absolute blessing. Yet for some of my congregation who were working in care homes at the beginning with not enough protective equipment, it was something like hell.

Liturgically we faced a challenge in that the Eucharist became something that you talked about rather than did together. The thing that still surprises me about a regular Sunday morning, in the middle of this city, is that people can walk into our church, and they eat and drink bread and wine for free, with other people they've never met before. Doing it together, rather than just talking about 'the night before he died', is really important. So the way flesh went back to words didn't make any sense to me at all. I subscribe to the notion that all celebrate the Eucharist. One presides on behalf of the community, but everyone present is a celebrant. When you're online, how does that make sense?

At St James's, we often say we're proud that William Blake was baptized at our church. As an aside, given his excoriating criticism of the church in his day, I think that was probably his first and last moment in the church; his entry and exit as it were. But in his concept that eternity is in one hour and heaven is in a wild flower, he's playing with perspective. That's what we're doing when we celebrate the Eucharist: we're jumping into a waterfall and immediately going out of our depth, drenched in this grace-filled moment, this sacrament. So the renewal of human living can be enacted in our eucharistic identity, which isn't a narrowly defined sacrament of the church, it's a way of living that is taking seriously our existence in eternity and our confinement for this moment in time. Rather than being a memorial service, the Eucharist is a future-oriented sacrament. It's showing us the future, as God wills it. And inviting us to live that future liturgically now.

Just as the bread and wine are transformed, we are also transformed, because we notice the kingdom among us – all are welcome, all are fed, no one is thirsty. The Eucharist is a fundamental celebration of who you are and who I am, together before God. And at the same time, in the life of Jesus that is narrated and also present in that sacrament, we're reminded of our capacity for betrayal, our need for mercy, our violence, our competitive instincts: we're faced with ourselves in a fundamental way, but in a way that we can bear. And then we're fed. So there's something really extraordinary about a Eucharist that shows you what human life could really be like, if we stepped into it and lived it. The ritualistic practice of Eucharist is a rehearsal for heaven at one level, at the same time as returning to the earthly altar where all are welcome, no one is left thirsty, and no one is left behind.

There's a lovely phrase from a poem, 'For Dudley', by the American Richard Wilbur: 'All that we do is touched with ocean', but we cannot step into it and leave what we know behind, what is on the shore. I've often thought that on a Sunday morning at our celebration of the Eucharist. The invitation is to remember that 'All that we do is touched by ocean, but we remain on the shore of what we know', but actually we do remain on the shore often, which means we get fussed about doing things right or who's sitting in that seat or who's moved in that way. If we're in this for anything, it's to expand and deepen and celebrate life as it can be. We're brilliant, as human beings, at continually confining, defining, shoving it into a box, into some kind of thing that we think we can know the beginning and the end of. We often use mystery as a catch-all full stop at the end of a sentence when we don't really know what we're talking about. But really to enter into the mystery of living – what it's really like to be alive – that's astonishing. To try to continue to say that in the middle of the pandemic has been hard, but that's been the unique vocation of a eucharistic community in this time.

As a priest, a lot of the time I haven't felt useful. I'm not a doctor. I'm not a scientist. I'm not a person who in this moment can help, genuinely help, to move society into a better place. Am I a front-line worker? I don't want to make this into a kind of more sharply expressed observation than it needs to be; although I did, as many others did, hold up phones to help people say goodbye to the people that they loved. But at the same time, certainly in the UK, there were some spectacular communities that really got going with their food banks. We fed people who were homeless. But fundamentally, across the UK, one of the truths that was revealed by the pandemic was that the church had to understand that there wasn't a universal turning to the church. There wasn't a cry, 'Why has God visited this on us? Let's go to the Church of England to find out why.' I think that realization has been very good for us. Because it's let us know that we are less regarded even than we thought we were. That's not to take away from a lay person I talked to who has been holding services in the churchyard of her local church; she just turned up in a graveyard and started reading out prayers: people came socially distanced and gathered, and they got on with it while the church was shut – fantastic. But as a whole, it's been a moment of reckoning. A philosopher said to me recently, if there were any moment where the church really could come into its own, do you not think it would be a global pandemic? And while people in churches have done a huge amount of helping their local communities, and that's been incredible, there hasn't been a universal turning to the church to understand what has been happening, and why it's been happening.

There's a bit of me that is quite proud of society for not doing that. Because that means people are thinking and they're not automatically going to come out of a sense of obligation or a fear of authority. Those days are very thankfully long gone, and I think that's a good, very good, thing. But this truth-telling lays down a challenge to a eucharistic community. How is God's invitation to live, really live, well, together, being lived out by us? If we can't communicate that, then no wonder people are having a look and wandering off. There's much that's good: the growth in craft, the growth in walking in woods – all of that is absolutely fantastic. I'm not complaining about that. But it has been a bit of a reckoning if clergy really thought they were key workers and front-line people. To some extent, of course, in certain circumstances, we have been there. But as a whole, the church often spends too much time providing answers to questions no one's asking, which is one of our greatest talents, often.

Some of our instincts are to try to do our absolute best and try hard not to be envious or worry about what we're not doing. That betrays a contemporary challenge for anyone trying to live a spiritual life, which is that there is so much to divert and distract us in modern living. There's so much opportunity for vacuous overactivity to fill whatever void it is that we've got. The church is not immune to that. If we're not careful, competition can enter every aspect of human life. Sara Maitland used to talk about competitive vulnerability in some of the feminist groups that she was part of in the 1970s. And there can be competitive creativity as well. Churches felt that they had to be seen to be responding well to the crisis. Who's that for? At whose service are we placing our creativity? At whose feet do we place our precious gifts of energy, ideas and solutions? It's easy for us to become idolatrous, and place our energy, creativity and gifts at the feet of an idol, which can be our own ego, individually or collectively. Those ancient teachings of faithfulness and idolatry are as relevant today as they were then, just in different ways.

I'm talking about motivation. To offer all that we have and all that we can be and do with our creativity is a fantastic thing. I want to emphasize that. But in whose service are we offering it? It should be a constant refrain for any church or church leader: 'In whose service am I expending this energy?' Or, 'In whose service am I working for this?' The chief spiritual discipline for priests, in a eucharistic sense, is not to think up the most amazing all-singing, all-dancing Eucharist on ice: the most important thing is to keep returning to the source of true creativity, which is God. For me as a priest it is that space behind the altar, which feels incredibly spacious, an uncreated place of renewal. So the chief spiritual discipline is not to run around but to return. In returning is the renewal of our strength. It's when I don't return that I get lost. It's when I don't go back to stand in the place of my first love, that's when I can get lost and angry and disorientated and exhausted by the demands of what turns out to be vacuous overactivity.

There have been pros and cons about online church. If you are fortunate enough to have stable Wi-Fi, and privacy, then it's made some people's homes a place of prayer in a way that they weren't before. For people with physical impairments, who may have found it quite difficult to access church buildings, or to travel to church, it's made churches more accessible in every possible way. But if you don't have stable Wi-Fi, or if you don't have privacy in your own space, then it has been harder to remain part of that community. One aspect of video conferencing has been that the breakout rooms on Zoom have been fantastic for us, I've heard many people say – to be put randomly in a room with three or four people that you have seen a bit, but you can't remember the names; the names are written on the screen, which is better. You can actually connect and make real relationships. Like many churches, we have coffee after the service, and courses and groups, as much as any other parish, but the breakout room element has deepened and transformed the relationships within the congregation. And that's been fantastic.

At St James's we've had a number of art installations and experimented with symbolic actions during the liturgy. One was by an artist in our congregation called Sarah Mark. To highlight the climate crisis, she filled an oil barrel with water, froze it, removed the ice inside the barrel, suspended it over the barrel, and then melted the ice into the oil barrel, placing a microphone in the bottom, so the sound was spread throughout the church. We celebrated the Eucharist and continued with all our normal services over the weekend in the presence of melting ice, real melting ice, and listening to it. We put it deliberately in the middle of the church to be a disruptive presence. There were some people who were pretty annoyed by having to go round it. But that's the point. The prayers we prayed were the same as before but the presence of melting ice changed their meaning. Before this all sounds unbearably worthy, there was a very good moment when we were installing it the night before. There were about three or four of us there, and we couldn't get the ice melted sufficiently to take it out of the oil barrel. So somebody just said, 'Well, we could just turn the boiler up for a short time!' It took a few seconds for all of us to realize that this was absolutely the wrong thing to do, given the point of the installation, and caused much laughter at our own hypocrisy. Those moments are really important in church life to help dispel hubris or smugness.

I keep remembering the line from the Magnificat that God has scattered the proud in the imagination of their hearts. Imagination is not enough in itself. You can be as imaginative as you like. It's the idolatry of service theme again. To take the church where I am now as an example, St James's as a congregation is a place where people believe and know themselves to be creative selves. That's something that was there long before I went there. I am simply riding that wave with them and am committed to harnessing our imagination faithfully in the service of God in mission. Imagination is a gift from God. But we need to recognize the source of that creativity and to whom it belongs. Imagination can be used to execute people or to hurt them or to divide us. So, imagination in, or creativity in, themselves are not necessarily of God unless we recognize where that creativity comes from and place it back in God's hands.

Sometimes all a priest can be is a permission-giver – although, often you don't think something needs your permission. But you can help to create that space that means people can be and do whatever is in them to be or do. For example, the Sunday before the first lockdown, St James's had launched a wheat-growing project in the courtyard. For completely unexpected reasons, during the church closure, I became a wheat farmer. I had to look after the wheat in a way that I never would have antici-pated before. Slightly surreal events followed: I was on the phone, getting instruction about how to thin the wheat: our church warden is a former wheat farmer. The symbolism of a grain of wheat that fell into the earth, and the growing of the wheat, was important for a dispersed congregation to follow the story and the progress of something creative and good. But there are hidden dangers here too: sometimes we can believe that if we've done something symbolic, then we've confronted injustice, or it has been fixed in some way. That is simply not true. The Black Lives Matter move-ment, for example, acknowledged the importance of symbolism regarding statues, for instance, but properly interrogated those kinds of symbolic actions to say that it's not enough. It's not enough. Actual change, actual equality, actual repentance and change in behaviour from white church leaders like me – that's the only place to start with this discussion. The symbolic side is important, but you have to keep bringing yourself back to saying, what actual change is needed, and how do I contribute? How do I become part of that movement of the Spirit, from chaos to order, and from Babel to Pentecost?

St James's congregation, led by people in the congregation, has chosen to start by reading together Ben Lindsay's book, *We Need to Talk About Race*. Fifty people signed up to do this. The group deliberately chose that particular book because, as it says in the subtitle, it's about Black experi-ence in a white-majority church, and we are a white-majority church. The Anglican Church globally is certainly not a white-majority church. So even to start with, it's important to take care about how majorities and minorities are described. We were talking recently about the way racism is a structural sin – and, for example, liberation theology will want to make sure that structural sin is named and identified as such. But racism is also a personal sin. To try to interrogate oneself about that, as a white person, has been a very important part of this, as far as I've been concerned: to learn to listen harder, and more than that, to be part of a movement that is together trying to make real change in our church. That requires not only naming the structural racism, but having the personal courage and commitment, one on one, or in a small group, to say stuff that you hadn't said before. I have been trying to learn this more deeply: and again that's where truth-telling, mercy and trust come back in.

The German theologian Dorothy Sölle, of whom I'm a great devotee, died in 2003. She talked about revolutionary patience. I found myself preaching about that quite a bit this year. Her insight has inspired and helped me personally and as a priest. Revolutionary patience has energy and spaciousness in it. There's an element of waiting, but it's not stagnant waiting. It's expecting revolution, or stimulating a revolutionary attitude to living. Patience is often couched in passive terms, but revolutionary patience is something you can cultivate in a prayer life that could really change things.

And along with that, I often hear religious practice in music terms. This pandemic has reinforced my sense that it's very important to commit to dissonance in religious practice, not just aim for harmony all the time, because I think it's how the world is. This translates straightforwardly into church music. I don't really like it when all music in a service resolves, because for most people in the world, life is not like that. If we can't bring that dissonance into a church, I don't know where we're going to listen to it. I don't necessarily mean the music you need tuning forks for, which was written in the mid-twentieth century, that's just difficult, and everyone's desperate for a tune after it. What I'm talking about is music that expresses the deep brokenness we all carry. This has to find expression in church, and one way to do that is to tolerate dissonance that doesn't always resolve. I have become more attuned to that. I want to find a way not only to listen to that, but to sing.

One way of understanding my role as a priest, for church and society, is, I think, to invite others to listen to the divine song being sung right now, knowing that you are invited to join it with your own voice. And if you're going to take some time to figure out what that song sounds like, that's great. You figure that out. But my conviction is that there is something for you to sing. It doesn't have to be pretty, and it doesn't have to resolve, and it doesn't have to be part of a cadence that tells you that everything is eventually going to be okay. It can be unfinished, and it can be harmonious or dissonant, as long as it's yours. And we'll sing it together.

10 June 2021

15

Anthony Reddie

Identity

A postcolonial approach to theology recognizes that empire, in all its various manifestations, has been a feature of human life for well over a millennium. The church has been at the epicentre of empire and imperialism – sometimes resisting and critiquing, sometimes colluding with it and benefiting from it. The iteration that shapes my life is the British Empire. At its peak, 24 per cent of the world was controlled by it. My parents and antecedents come from the Caribbean island of Jamaica. There's a continuing relationship between those various parts of the world and Britain. Part of the dialectic of it – and the intellectual struggle around understanding the term – is that empires come to an end, and so in the second half of the twentieth century Britain either gave up those parts of the Empire voluntarily or was encouraged to walk away from them through political and military struggle, but a lot of the ideas that determined empire are still with us. They've embedded themselves into theology, into the way we see the world, into what we perceive as normal or as transgressive.

How do those perspectives continue to shape the world? Take the England football team. I saw an image on social media of the team, and it says, 'the England team without immigration', and points out the three or four white British players. This is a team which is very reflective of modern Britain. But for some people this is a problem. They'd love to go back to the good old days, when we were still a great imperial power. That contestation over how we imagine modern Britain is central to notions of postcolonialism. The past has gone, but its ideas are still embedded in our society and in our church. We think *post* means *beyond* or *after*. But postcolonialism doesn't mean colonialism is behind us. It indicates the relationship and the slippage between that past and this present, the way colonialism still shapes our consciousness. What does it mean to be British? What are the markers of belonging to Britishness? And what, then, is the role of faith and identity?

A lot of my work is narrative-driven – it's about the stories we tell, how we think of ourselves as human subjects. I'm born and brought up in Bradford, West Yorkshire. I still have a Yorkshire accent, even though I've lived in Birmingham for 38 years – they say you can take the man out of Yorkshire, but you can't take Yorkshire out of the man. I still call myself a Bradfordian, even though I don't live there. Postcolonialism is about that kind of negotiation between where we come from and where we are, between *root* and *route*. Identity involves that fluidity, continuity and change, which is played out in us as individuals, but also on a macro scale, in the context of what it means to be a nation. For example, when we celebrate St George's Day, or the Queen's Birthday, or other historic moments in the life of the country, it's simultaneously a contemporary event and it's drawing upon deep historical roots and cultural memory. Those two elements are always being contested.

Nostalgia has a huge impact on how this plays out. I romanticize growing up in Bradford, but the truth is that I live a comfortable middle-class life now in Birmingham, which is much better than where I came from. But if you ask me where I belong, I go back to an identity rooted in history, which is both mine and not mine. That's the power of myth. As Christians, we know how powerful myths and stories can be – how it's not always about whether a story is necessarily true, but about what it tells us about ourselves: how do myths generate meaning? We wrestle a lot with myths within the corporate identity of being British. We still think back to World War Two and that plucky sense of the British fighting against the Nazis. People of an older generation will often say that it was a happier time, a simpler time – when you could leave your door unlocked and community was stronger and people were friendly and connected to each other. I suspect there's a lot of truth in that. But if you ask people if they would want to go back to that period, most of us would not. Postcolonialism tries to wrestle with all of those dynamics: how we reconcile all our plural identities, how we're rooted in a particular place and time but with a past that lives with us still, in powerful and often deeply unhelpful ways.

We can see this powerfully in the church. Kierkegaard said that life is lived forward but understood backwards: we create identities by looking backwards at the direction from which we have come. When I was younger, it was often said that what it means to be human is to imagine who we are as we walk into the future. But that's not true – as human beings, what we actually do is to walk slowly into the future, facing backwards. In our Christian faith, we're shaped by tradition and scripture, both of which belong to the past. We're shaped by a story of history which we believe will shape our future. One of the reasons the church struggles with modernity, and now postmodernity, is that all our stories are of a past when the church was bigger, more important, more significant in people's lives and on the global stage.

I grew up in a city-centre mission built in 1872, at the latter end of the Victorian era when Methodism was growing exponentially. There was a sense of hubris in the Methodism of that time – having come out of the Church of England and feeling a real sense of purpose. This city-centre mission was a huge chapel seating 1,500 people, a monument to Non-conformism, deliberately opposite the Anglican cathedral. But even by the time it was built, it was already obsolete. Growing up in the 1970s and '80s in that church, I heard all about those days when there was a revival and the church was full – and it was pure mythology; the church was never full. But we told ourselves that, in those days, you had to turn up half an hour early to the service or you wouldn't get a seat and people were swinging from the balconies to hear the preaching. So, I grew up with a sense that the present is unsure and the future is scary – but what a fantastic past.

That's not just true of that particular church, or of Methodism – it's a difficulty that the whole church has, looking at our present and our future in the light of that 'glorious' history, which wasn't all that glorious if we really look. When we struggle with contemporary life, there's a struggle to go into the past, to re-imagine it, to believe that it will give us resources for the future. Sometimes that's true, because there are invariably parts of our history that we can recover and learn from. But we struggle to deal with that problem of redefinition. Even though we believe in resurrection, we don't want to die to get there. Of course we have a fear of death. What we really want is resuscitation – for God to pump a bit of life into the existing body. Whereas, really, we might need to die in our present incarnation for a new body to be resurrected. We don't know what they will look like, which is another reason we cling to the past – because it's what we know. It's comfortable and it's secure. How often do you hear the words, 'That's just how we do it around here'. And you want to reply, 'Yes, that's how you've been doing it and it hasn't been working for a long time.'

Growing up in that congregation in Bradford, mine was one of only two Black families. The real existential moment for me came when I was 11. I was in Sunday school, in a room right at the back of the church, and there was a picture of Jesus with piercing blue eyes, long blond hair and a beard. I asked the Sunday school teacher, 'Miss, Jesus is the son of God, he represents who God is. And we're all created in the image and likeness of God.' And she said, 'Yes.' And I asked, 'So then who am I?' There was a long silence. And she said, 'It doesn't matter, Anthony.'

That was an unsatisfying answer. On one level, she was right that it didn't matter. I was born into a family that said God had no colour and God loved everybody. In fairness, I never had any sense that I was not loved by God; I never had any sense I was not a member of the body of Christ. But in another sense it did matter. This was a racist church – the people were racist, not because they were terrible people but because that was the culture of the time. And I was bought up into that evangelical, Nonconformist, imperial vision of the church – a kind of internalized colonization. Then I went to the University of Birmingham and did a degree in church history and got involved in the Student Christian Movement, and with the chaplains, who began to politicize me a bit. My faith became more radical, but it was still white.

The real transformation, to a more contextual theology, came when I began to work as a church youth worker in some of the oldest Black communities in Birmingham, where people from the *Windrush* generation settled first in bedsits and then in their own houses. I worked for two Black-majority Methodist churches, where most of the congregation came from Jamaica and St Kitts and Nevis. My job was to work with the children and grandchildren who were connected to the church and the wider community. In that context, I started to ask, 'Where is God in this? What is God doing in the midst of this poverty and generational social alienation?' Most of the young people I worked with did not gain anything in the way of qualifications. There were two grammar schools, right in the centre of this conurbation, King Edward's Boys' School and King Edward's Girls' School. Their pupils were bussed in from other parts of the city. Most locals would never set foot inside those big school walls, like they were foreign territory in the middle of this community. I began to reflect that churches were doing good work keeping people going, giving them a sense of hope in the face of all the social forces that were against them, but they weren't saying anything prophetic about the context they were rooted in. Why were children from nice, white, leafy suburbs bussed into a school in this area, but virtually no one in the area itself would ever set foot in that school? Because there was the eleven-plus, which was almost impossible to pass if you were Black and working class. Why was that never seen as a problem? Why did no one even talk about it?

Then I had a fateful moment – 19 August 1992, I still remember it clearly. I was talking to my supervisor, the superintendent minister. He said, 'Anthony, we've got some money in our budget and we think you should do some vocational training. There's a man called Robert Beckford who's just started a course in Black theology at the Queen's Foundation. Here's a flyer; go along and see if you're interested.' So, I went to the taster class and on the handout there was an extract on Black liberation theology. It was like a light bulb going off in my head. I fell in love with Black theology in that moment. I bought all these books by James Cone and all these South African Black theologians. And then the question became, 'This is fantastic, but I'm not African American or South African. What does Black theology look like in Britain?'

I have a huge amount in common with African American theologians. Their theological agenda has very much informed my own. The fundamental difference between Black theology in the United States and in Britain isn't fundamentally about theological ideas but about different contexts for doing theology. In America, Black theology comes out of the African American experience of people who were slaves. James Cone talks about his experience of lynching, of being at the receiving end of visceral white supremacy. He talks about the fear of growing up with a father who was an activist for desegregation in a small town in the American South where the Ku Klux Klan were active – the fear that one day his father wouldn't come home. That history, and particularly the histories of slavery and segregation, clearly informs how Black theology talks about race in the American context. One of Cone's essays is called 'Theology's Great Sin: Silence in the Face of White Supremacy'. He says that America is founded on genocide of indigenous Native peoples on one hand and the importation of enslaved Africans on the other. That's how America was created – and throughout that, the church said nothing, white theologians said nothing, so that's their great sin.

In the British context, most Black and Asian people come from migrant families – Black people have been here since Roman times, but the majority of Black British people came over with the *Windrush*. My family's story is rooted in the Caribbean. It's still a story about our relationship with Britain, but it's not grounded in shared physical space in the way it is in the United States. My parents' generation felt like their homes here were transitory, so making provision for a long-term stay wasn't part of their consciousness. When I was growing up, I talked about 'back home' in Jamaica, even though I'd never been there. In Britain, the demographics of Black and Asian marginalization are very similar to America. White supremacy has marginalized us in the same way. Yet there's been no segregation, no laws to say that Black people can't buy a house in this area. It's all been done in more subtle ways, through economics and through custom. When I write my version of Black theology, I'm not James Cone. I haven't experienced segregation enacted through law – which doesn't mean that we haven't experienced segregation in Britain, only that its dynamics are different. The categories of race and class have been constructed in different ways. Contextualized Black theology in Britain focuses much more on what it means to be a migrant, negotiating your identity in relation to empire.

In Britain we've also had a much stronger sense of coalition. When I write about Black theology, I'm partly writing out of an African, and in my case African Caribbean, perspective but I'm also including Asian people. Because what we have in common is that all of us are immigrants who come from the Empire – from India, Pakistan, Bangladesh, Africa and the Caribbean. The history of racialization and anti-racism in Britain has given us this strong sense of coalition. In America, Black theology really means African American theology. So doing Black theology with a British accent is different.

There's often a contested relationship between Black liberation theology and this broader project of Christianity. It's contested because colonialism is built into Christianity. There's a point in church history, with the conversion of Constantine, where Christianity goes from being a dissident movement in underground catacombs to being a part of the Roman Empire. Long before the British Empire came on to the scene, our faith was already implicated by imperialism. Postcolonial scholars, like myself, have to wrestle with that question of whether we can deconstruct the faith to the point that we can extricate ourselves from empire. I'm not entirely sure if we can. If you imagine a bruised piece of fruit and you peel away the skin and cut out the bruised parts, if you're not careful, you've cut away so much that you haven't got any fruit left. It's such a big part of our history – this is a faith 2,000 years old, and about 1,600 of those have been spent sitting at the top table in the position of power. Take the divine right of kings: that's a classic conflation of empire and Christian faith. Yet for all of that, at the heart of our faith is this dissident rabbi, a Palestinian Jew, who is the opposite of empire. He's fighting a revolution – a revolution that understands that authentic revolutionary change starts with the heart and moves outwards.

If we think about revolution in humanistic terms, we think about first overthrowing the overall structure and hoping that we can bring people along with us, which doesn't bring about authentic change. What tends to happen is that violence begets violence and the new group in charge ends up being just as barbaric as the one that came before. You end up in this cycle where power isn't actually deconstructed. Jesus' revolution of love is about creating a systemic, epistemological change, a transformation of how we understand knowledge and truth and self. It gives us a way of being human that's not tied to aggrandisement, privilege and power – but rather to servanthood and love for each other. That's what keeps Black liberation and postcolonial theologians in this broad tent of Christianity. I remain faithful to it because, for all its messiness and continual disappointments, I see the creative sparks of renewal which come from a God who is always improvising, always challenging us to change, and who is incarnate in the radical figure of Jesus whose life was against empire.

I get my students to read the passage in the Gospels where Jesus is before Pilate. Jesus is being asked all these questions and they're trying to trap him into incriminating himself, but he's giving elusive answers. Then, Pilate says, 'What is truth?' When we read that, as a church, we identify with Jesus, but in the context of the history of Christendom, we're more often Pilate. When we think about empire and the power we possess, that's where we sit. None of my students want to identify with Pilate. But while we're critiquing him, we're doing it from within the system he represents, at the heart of a former imperial power. Part of the challenge of postcolonial theology is recognizing that, for the bulk of our history, British churches have been more representative of Pilate than of Jesus. We need to be able to recognize the embedded way in which we have been part of the problem before we can be part of the solution.

What gives us hope, however, is that the Jesus we read about in the Gospels is constantly challenging us, nudging us, sometimes shouting at us, saying, 'You can be different. Let me show you how.' That same Jesus is alive whenever two or three of us gather as a church, every time we celebrate the Eucharist. His radicalism is made manifest through the Eucharist. That gives us a means of going out and being different, critiquing Pilate, and asking him to repent. To speak truth to power is not arrogance or self-righteousness. We have to say with humility and gentleness, but nonetheless with conviction, that what the church and the world perceive as normal is not the kingdom.

For much of the history of Christendom, there was a tendency to think of empire as providential and coterminous with the kingdom – the idea that society as we know it is what God wants the world to look like. Not that everything about our society is terrible; I'm a creature of it. The only reason I'm able to speak on this is because people perceive me as having something worth hearing, because of my education and my position – ensconced in the University of Oxford, which is hardly a bastion of revolutionary change. I have to wear my revolutionary credentials lightly because I'm still a creature of empire. But I still believe that at the heart of this contested, problematic institution called the church, and this problematic phenomenon called Christianity, is a prophetic God who tells us that the first will be last and the last will be first, that all of us in the body of Christ are important and valuable in God's economy, and that God's place is with those on the margins. I love that John Wesley said to the early Methodists, 'Don't go to those who need you, go to those who need you the most.' There's a tradition within the church, not just within liberation theology, of God's preferential option for those who are on the margins and those who are oppressed.

8 July 2021

16

Ben Quash

Perception

In my journey towards the arts, there have been two significant milestones. The first was during my English degree – studying for the exhilaratingly ambitious paper on literary tragedy, which was (and still is) the lynchpin of the course: the final summit we all had to ascend. The wonderful thing about the tragedy paper is that it focuses on the texts of literary tragedy as well as their performance history. It's deliberately set up to drive you towards the biggest existential questions that you can ask. It's effectively a paper in metaphysics, and raises all kinds of philosophical questions about what sort of a world we live in: Can we be at home in a world like this? How do we account for suffering? What role do non-human agents like the gods of Greek tragedy have in our lives and the dilemmas we face?

I was already a worshipping Christian and beginning to explore a possible vocation to ordained ministry when that tragedy paper carried me towards theology. When I eventually came to do my PhD in theology, my first question to my supervisor was about how I could combine my theological interests with the things that excited me from the tragedy paper. He replied that I should study Hans Urs von Balthasar, the twentieth-century Swiss Catholic theologian, famous for his 15-volume work of systematic theology – the central part of which is five volumes on drama.

Having become a Balthasarian scholar, for better or worse, I began to read more of his work, beyond the volumes on drama, particularly the first seven volumes which he subtitles *A Theological Aesthetics*. In those volumes he begins to engage, in various ways, with visual experience and how we can explore the fact of God's self-revelation by analogy with visual experience: how one's eyes may be literally opened to God. In a volume called *Seeing the Form*, he draws on medieval theological texts exploring aesthetic experience. Revelation, in this tradition, involves a combination of light and form. If you have form without illumination, you see nothing – you have form, but in darkness. By the same token, when light has nothing to strike against or shine through, it is invisible to the eye. By analogy, revelation is the process of created objects – created by God – becoming luminous through revelation. The light of their divine origin communicates itself through them. It is in their particularity, combined with the infinite depth and infinite light of God, that we encounter revelation.

Before I knew it, then, Balthasar had taken me into aesthetics: that's the second milestone. There was a further stop on the way, however, in my encounter with Caravaggio. Two years before I came to King's College London, there was a major exhibition at the National Gallery on Caravaggio's work. Scholars have speculated endlessly on Caravaggio's religious views, which are ultimately unknowable, but my own conviction is that for all his turbulent and sullied life – maybe because of his turbulent and sullied life – he painted grace. He understood sin and grace. His canvases are depictions of a profound struggle between light and darkness, expressions of his own experience of struggle, and they are extraordinary. They are full of Christian seriousness – sometimes doubt, sometimes lack of conviction, but within which we see another kind of conviction at work, not so much confessional as existential. Caravaggio was the final step towards a complete fascination with the visual arts, not just aesthetics in the rather more elevated Balthasarian, theoretical sense, but actual works of art: the way they can immerse and change you.

When I began my post as Professor of Christianity and the Arts at King's, I was in the wonderful position of occupying a newly created post. Universities were very different places in 2007: before the financial crash, before student fees really kicked in and changed the whole culture of higher education. There was a freedom to the post – 'arts' defined in the plural, a blank canvas. The one clear guideline, especially for a university at the heart of London with theatreland on its doorstep, was to form partnerships with arts institutions in the city.

The first serious approach I made was to Nick Penny, who was then director of the National Gallery, who invited me to lunch at the Gallery. It was the only time in my life where a lunch has resulted in a decision that changed my life. This sounds like a testimony to the Holy Spirit at work, which is not my normal style. But because of that lunch, we created an MA programme at King's, run in collaboration with the National Gallery, which has now been running for over ten years. That sealed my commitment to the visual arts – call it serendipity, call it contingency, call it the work of the Holy Spirit. I hadn't planned, until then, to lead with the visual arts; it was more that they found me. They found a way to enter into this flowering of conversation with theology.

As we launched the MA, the National Gallery had an exhibition called 'Devotion by Design', which was all about altarpieces. That exhibition exemplified two ways of engaging with sacred art by using two types of gallery space. As you moved through the exhibition, you began with a room exploring the material of altarpieces – how they were made, the technical skills of the artists, the role of patronage – how the raw material of the works might tell us something of their history. Then you progressed to a room which was effectively the reconstruction of a church.

It was the first time the National Gallery, and probably any major international art museum, had done anything like that. One of the curators of that exhibition was Jennifer Sliwka, now my colleague at the Visual Commentary on Scripture. A trained art historian, she worked to restore the altarpieces to positions that echoed the way they would have been experienced by those who first encountered them in churches. There were side altars along the perimeter of the room, and a high altar at the East end with a beautiful altarpiece over it, and candlesticks and Gregorian chant: a bit ersatz, but a very powerful experience. It created an opportunity for visitors to the gallery to think about these objects not only as participating in the story of art, which is how they are normally presented in galleries, but as part of a much bigger conversation: the story of faith and the history of the church. Given that galleries can't just plonk their sacred works of art back into churches, their responsibility as custodians is to give people the context and the opportunity to engage with them – to feel their impact, not just to observe them as normal physical objects, or as historical sources which can tell us about who had the power to commission such things, and changing economic relationships in the past, but as religious objects.

Good works of art are themselves conversational. In Caravaggio's *The Calling of St Matthew*, Christ holds out his finger as he summons Levi, the tax collector, to become Matthew. So far as its finger in composition is concerned, the painting is an echo of the finger of God on the ceiling of the Sistine Chapel. So Jesus is acting in this situation as the creator: bringing Matthew into being where there was only Levi. But the *shape* of the hand is that of the Sistine Chapel's *Adam*. Jesus, who is both divine and human, is doing the works of God in creaturely flesh. Theologically, that is just a stroke of genius! It's a brilliant exploration of the hypostatic union of the divine and human nature. It's also a conversation with Michelangelo. It's out of an artistic conversation that a new theological insight can emerge.

The conversations in which you find yourself opening up to someone deeply or finding someone opening up deeply to you are often not when you face each other across a table. Rather, it's when you sit side by side with someone, such as on a long car journey, that you can communicate most honestly. There's something about being jointly turned towards something else, which might be the unfolding road in front of you as you drive or might be a work of art. Maybe the confessional is like this, too. It allows a divine and certain opening up of the self. I think the arts more generally do that, not just the visual arts.

Art is generous in the way it permits you to start talking. I find this with our students on the Master's programme when we're in the gallery. We begin by just standing in front of a painting and asking, 'What do you see?' It's about the simplest question you can ask. And whatever they choose is already the beginning of a conversation. If their eye was drawn to somebody's sword hilt or the light shining through an upper window in a corner of the painting, or a cat looking greedily at a bird, whatever it is, they've taken the first step. If you keep going with it, it leads you into more substantive discussion, which usually washes up on the shores of theology. But starting simply allows the conversation to be less threatening, more permissive.

I'm convinced that the arts are the most wonderful gateway to theological questions – whereas if you start with God or sin or other weighty theological concepts, people often just shut down. Sometimes the conversation involves a direct line of influence. Caravaggio was painting in Rome and he could see Michelangelo's work, but the dialogue between their paintings isn't limited to that. Works of art can talk quite unexpectedly to each other. Out of those encounters or collisions, catalytic moments can generate new insight. Somebody like Albrecht Dürer can make an engraving of the supper at Emmaus and give it a sort of pyramidal structure: Christ presiding at one end of the table, the two disciples who walked with him sitting lower down, and a glass sitting on the table displaying what's called a conical kick: a little mountain inside the glass that helps to strengthen it. And these structures within the work, whether or not Dürer intended them to do so, recall an icon of the transfiguration. The mountain of the transfiguration suddenly speaks to the conical kick in the glass at the centre of a pyramid structure, where Christ is again revealing the light of his glory to new eyes at the supper as he breaks bread. That's works of art talking theology to each other. You could do that by putting a very contemporary work, like a Damien Hirst cow sliced in half, next to something like the expulsion from Eden, perhaps with a reflection on what separation means, and you'll be emotionally and theologically engaged with questions that are profound.

One of the biggest inspirations for the Visual Commentary on Scripture was the way collections of patristic commentaries were collected in manuscripts during the Middle Ages, bringing together lots of different perspectives on biblical texts in one place. Scribes copied and compiled different texts by authors from different places and points in time, placing them next to each other and inevitably bringing them into conversation. They don't always agree, but they converse, and that means you get a sense of the rich texture of interpretation that arises from the biblical text.

I don't think God gave us the Bible in order that we could turn it into a set of agreed propositions that everybody signed off on. God gave us the Bible to talk about – the conversation is one of its gifts. The conversation forms a community. A group of people don't need to agree to be a community, they just need to talk to each other. The Jewish tradition does the same thing with the Talmud – conversations between rabbis are preserved in complex composite pages, read for centuries afterwards, still available for us to read today. That's an encouragement to us as we try to create conversations between multiple artworks and contributors.

The difficulty here is that some people have historically been missing from the conversation. As we developed the Visual Commentary on Scripture, this has proved a huge practical challenge – how to find works of art beyond the mainstream Old Master tradition of Western Europe, much of which was then exported in various kinds of colonial expansion and provided the prototypes for imitative works of art in other parts of the world. Works of art outside that tradition are harder to find: they're not front and centre in our museums, they don't come up on the first page of Google search results. But Christians are all over the world worshipping every day with material artefacts, visual artefacts that are profoundly integrated with their life of faith and their devotion, and which are beautiful in ways people in the West have yet to fully appreciate. Then there is the question of what we allow to be called art – particularly in the case of everyday objects embedded into the ordinary fabric of domestic space, which are at the same time forms of creative, imaginative artistry.

One object we've featured is a horrific object and not a work of art by any conventional measure. It's a metal headpiece with a spike that fits into the mouth, called a scold's bridle. In the early modern period it was used against women who were seen to be talking or gossiping too much. We featured it next to a passage from the Epistle of James. It's a deeply shocking, disturbing object, and a very powerful object to bring into conversation with a passage about taming the tongue.

The works of Christian art you find on the walls of the National Gallery and other fine art museums mainly depict narrative scenes. They are stories of Jesus and saints from the Gospels and Acts, or stories from the sagas and chronicles of the Old Testament/Hebrew Bible. But if you look at everyday objects – for example, jugs from Puritan homes in sixteenth- and seventeenth-century England, which were often engraved with biblical verses – you find completely different parts of the Bible:

Psalms, Proverbs, wisdom literature, passages that people used to steer their everyday lives, negotiating life with the wisdom of the Bible at hand. Those are just as important and illuminating as the narratives that are taken up in fine art.

The key criteria for the Visual Commentary on Scripture are that the artworks or objects we choose should converse well with other works of art and should reward repeated contemplation. Sometimes works of art in any medium are one-trick wonders. They make a quick impact, but you don't feel any need to come back to them. This has a lot to do with the way people engage with art, especially online, where you can scroll past a Rembrandt on Instagram without really registering it. It's regrettable that works that could keep on giving aren't given the opportunity – because we don't take the opportunity to really look at them.

In advertising, you can reach people by push or by pull. Push advertising is slightly coercive: it tries to make you buy the product by telling you that you fail if you don't own it. Pull advertising, meanwhile, works by awakening your desire. There are theologies and ways of preaching that work a lot like push advertising – it's prescriptive, it tells you what you need to do – and in our present culture there is a great hostility to the church speaking to the world in this way. That's not me saying that I don't think there's a place for ethics or even for denunciation, but I think as a general strategy it's not a good one for encouraging people to engage with the church. It closes the conversation before it starts. Whereas there's something about art that draws you forward, invites you, elicits response. Response is all about being conjured out of yourself and enlarging your world, carrying you out of the habits of daily life which are increasingly micromanaged and confined and compartmentalized. It takes you somewhere expansive where you can connect all the different dimensions of your life against the biggest horizon you can imagine. And, otherwise, what's the point? Why clock in and out on time every day at work if you never ask the bigger questions? That's what the church should be doing anyway; and it can do it powerfully with art if it harnesses those possibilities.

We should approach art with an adventuring spirit, expecting to find and be changed by wonderful things, and often profoundly disturbing things, too. In being drawn forward, we can be confident that we're not just scrambling around in what we already know and have already encountered. That our eschatological horizon is open and exciting, and that its fulfilment will be in being drawn to Christ, who is the true centre of everything.

9 September 2021

17

Brian McLaren
Transformation

During the Covid-19 lockdown, I've felt more acutely how privileged I am. I have a place to live. I'm financially stable. I've had the luxury, during lockdown, of not needing to go out and risk my life to keep a salary coming in. I feel a newfound empathy for those who have no choice but to go out and risk their lives every day: to show up at the hospital or to show up at the grocery store – to help the public at risk to themselves. On top of that, I have quick access to medication, vaccines and so on. Many of us thought of the lockdown as a terrible limitation, but then we begin to realize what a privilege we have – to be able to isolate from a dangerous virus, and to know that medical help is available to us. I feel all the more how with privilege comes responsibility, and with great privilege (to quote Spiderman) comes great responsibility.

On my side of the Atlantic, the pandemic put on display how religion, and in our case the Christian religion, can be deeply dysfunctional and sick, even dangerous, even deadly. I think of all the pastors who put their congregations in danger, all to make sure they had a crowd to adore them for another week. I think of all those Christians who have fallen prey to conspiracy theories – people who have been the first to fall for crazy, ignorant fantasies. Don't you think this reveals some serious failure in our Christian faith – the fact that we haven't protected people from conspiratorial foolishness, that we haven't vaccinated them with wisdom that would protect them from fools and charlatans who want to take advantage of them? I can't help but think that the anti-science bias is so deeply ingrained in many sectors of Christian communities. People oppose Darwin for 150 years, and you might think, 'Oh, well, that's too bad, but what harm does it do?' But then you see, at a time like this, how opposing science is deadly, when it not only makes you vulnerable to getting sick but also to infecting others and harming them. I can't help but feel that the lessons of this pandemic could prepare us for the realities of climate change, but sadly very few, especially among pious, zealous church folk, have learned the lessons. So I come out of this period with an increased willingness to take risks and try to say what needs to be said within the Christian community, because we need a vital alternative to the kind of backward and destructive Christianity that's functioning out there in so many millions of hearts and minds.

Many of us remember singing the hymn 'Faith of our fathers'. There was this sense that faith was primarily about staying loyal to the past. We had to keep saying what they said in the past and doing what they did in the past. We had a deep obligation to remain anchored in the past. But that's made us highly irresponsible in relation to loyalty to the future and responsibility to the future. I think of the difference between this and the indigenous vision. Many of our indigenous people here in my country said their primary ethical directive is to think of the effect of their actions seven generations into the future. Meanwhile, in my white Christian culture, my ethical obligation to my descendants is almost invisible. Many of our doctrines of the end times (our eschatologies) feed into this ethical failure. We think, 'Well, isn't Jesus coming soon? Isn't the world going to be destroyed soon, and then we'll all go to heaven?' This mindset further obliterates any deep feeling of obligation to the future. Sadly, so many are ignorant of a powerful movement in theology, seen in theologians in Germany like Wolfhart Pannenberg and Jürgen Moltmann, or in process theologians in the US like John Cobb and Sr Ilia Delio, and especially in the Black theology of Howard Thurman and Barbara Holmes and the liberation theology of Jon Sobrino and Leonardo Boff. Instead of there being a sense that God is in the past, shooting off the big bang, which propels us into the future, these theologies of hope and liberation say, 'Let's imagine God is in the future, as the totality of good possibilities in the future. God is sending us the present moment from the future.' In other words, the future is the repository of time, and it's flowing to us, passing through us and every incoming moment of possibility. We have an option to choose what's better, or choose what's worse; choose what's wise, or what's foolish. That theological vision is so liberating and revolutionary that we could say it reverses the polarity of the universe. Instead of being driven from behind, we're being invited into the future. The future begins to matter more and more.

I think of salmon at the end of their life. They're getting old or tired. Most of their life is behind them. But that is when they do their most creative act, which is to swim up the rivers and end their life laying and fertilizing eggs and creating the future of their species. Many pastors and denominations have become so rigid and nostalgic. Rather than being bold like salmon, they've become so cowardly in the sense that they don't want to say or do anything that will upset their major donors. But thank God for those pastors who say, 'I'm going to risk everything, and

I'm going to try to lead our congregation into a new relationship to the world, focused on the future. I'm going to reverse the polarity of our congregational universe.' So it's happening among some pastors. It's also happening among people who have dropped out, but can't hide the fact that the Spirit of God has touched them, and the life and teaching of Jesus have inspired them. So they haven't been able to find a church where there's any place for them. But they're forming little connections and communities, some of them on Zoom, spread around the world, and yet they're encouraging each other and welcoming this vision of the future.

In my 2019 book, *Faith after Doubt*, I talked about people progressing through various stages of faith. When you pass from one stage to the next, doubt is the portal: you have to doubt your current stage to give you the motivation to seek something better. In the early stages of faith, many of us are given a very rigid system of beliefs. Our preoccupation becomes, how do I get an even more perfect system of beliefs? Many of us spend decades of our lives in a quest for belief perfection, as if beliefs were our salvation. Now, I'm all for upgrading our beliefs. But eventually, I think what people realize is, we're never going to have the perfect system of beliefs; and even if we did, we'd never be able to convince more than three other people to sign up to it. That's why for me, and for growing numbers of us, Christian faith is increasingly about a way of life rather than a system of beliefs. Then we make a critical decision: we aren't going to wait for people above us in the hierarchy, or a majority of people around us, to agree with us. We just say, I have no choice, I have to live into this future, as I am, starting right now.

We see this courage blooming everywhere. Among Catholics, we see it in Pope Francis. You can be sure that if he weren't the pope, he would not just be a standard toe-the-line Catholic. He would be thinking in ways that would shake things up, turning the church from its obsession with the past to a vision for the future. In so doing, of course, he is upsetting people who feel that God truly is more interested in preserving the past than in creating a better future. As a result, many of his own bishops are his strongest opponents. But many Catholics, especially poor Catholics, stand with Francis. I think of a Catholic woman to whom my wife and I are close, a neighbour who doesn't have proper documentation. She's just trying to live out this future-oriented vision in her very quiet life on the margins. What the pope and this humble woman who makes her living cleaning houses have in common is this commitment not to wait for anybody else, but to start living into that future right now.

I used to think that this obsession with the past was a uniquely Christian problem. But now I'm realizing it's a human problem. We see it in government and politics. We see it in economics and business. We see it in education and entertainment. People keep repeating old scripts, living as if the status quo were the only option, living as if what we're currently doing is sustainable.

I think the message of the New Testament is an invitation to stop looking back and instead rethink everything so a new future can be possible. We see it in Jesus, of course, as he speaks of good news, a message of a new kingdom, using images of new birth, new wine, new life, a new covenant or arrangement. It's there in Paul as well; he is constantly speaking of a new humanity in Christ, and the sense that we can walk into a new way of being human, participating in the birth of a new creation.

People often ask me about the future shape of church. I feel I know less about that now than I did 15 or 20 years ago, because we're in this period of profound reorganization of all of human life. At its most fundamental, the entire human species has to find a new way of living with the earth: a new way of living with time and the reality of death, of living with our ethical responsibility to future generations. We're in the process of reorganizing all these very basic things. I don't expect that to be a short-term process, or a clean and neat process. It's going to take a long time. There's unavoidable stress between here and there. So we have to trust the long arc of God's work in the world. We have to trust in a longer picture, and let go of the idea that we're going to fix this in time for the next annual meeting or through the next election. Imagine we could go back in time to January 2020, and all of us have a conversation with ourselves and say, 'Listen, in two months, there's going to be news of this pandemic. And here's how it's going to change your life.' I don't suppose any of us would have believed it. And if we'd been told, 'And it's going to last a couple of years', we would think that's impossible. But through the turmoil of the pandemic, we've shown ourselves our capacity for resilience, our ability to adjust. We've proved to ourselves how adaptable we can be. And those are exactly the practices we're going to need going forward. It's that attitude of resilience and the ability to recognize we might be in a rough patch for quite a long time. That's when we're able to draw from the resources of our faith, the ability to be resilient and persistent. That word endurance comes up so much in the New Testament. It's a quality we're going to need in spades going forward.

I sometimes say the form of Christianity I was inducted into was an evacuation plan: the earth is doomed, and here's the escape pod to get to heaven. My whole life and theology changed when I started to realize that in the Lord's Prayer, we don't pray, 'Our Father who art in heaven, hallowed be thy name, may we go to heaven as soon as possible where your kingdom is', but rather, 'May your will be done on earth, may your kingdom come on earth.' So the gospel is actually a transformation plan, about joining God and God's dreams and wishes and hopes for a desired future on earth. It's one of the things I think becomes obvious when you study church history. And if you live long enough, you even see it in your own lifetime. Here's the truth: the journey never ends. Things are never fully and finally fixed. Yesterday's solutions create today's problems, for which we need new solutions tomorrow, and so on. We love to project on to the Bible 'happily ever after' endings. We read the Bible as if the Promised Land leads to 'happily ever after'. If we can just get through this wilderness, we think, we'll be in the Promised Land and all will be well for ever. But when I read the Bible, I find that the Promised Land isn't 'they lived happily ever after'. Yes, the Promised Land is better than slavery. It's probably better than the wilderness. But you've got the Assyrians and the Egyptians and the Babylonians and the Philistines all trying to steal some of your milk and honey. So having a Promised Land doesn't solve everything.

So then the prophets start imagining a promised time. In Isaiah, and in many of the other prophets, when they start dreaming of this promised time, it's no longer just about them. It's no longer just about Israel. They realize if Israel is going to have a good future, Egypt needs a good future, and the Philistines need a good future and the Assyrians need a good future. Because otherwise, we're going to be afraid our neighbour is going to rob some of our milk and honey because they're starving. So you start to see this vision expand from a Promised Land to a promised time; and you don't get the feeling that that promised time is all roses, either. The promised time that you can envision at this moment is a breakthrough from our current problems. But in all likelihood, when we get to that breakthrough, some new problems will arise. And what that says to me is that we need a vision, not of struggle and then resolution, but a vision of continuing growth, continuing maturity – continuing evolution, if you will. Years ago, someone encouraged me to read more about Gregory of Nyssa, one of the early church's theological geniuses. Gregory of Nyssa got in trouble with his fellow clergy, because he didn't believe there was a state of perfection. He said perfection is infinite progression. He believed every creative thing is called to continual growth. He didn't envision an arrival, but ongoing, unending growth. I think he had an insight we all need.

I have come to believe that very little of the New Testament is focused on the afterlife. When Jesus speaks of the kingdom of God, I don't think that means heaven after you die. I think he's talking about a new way of living that involves God's will being done on earth, as in heaven. When I say God's will, I don't mean God's dominating and imposing tyrannical rule. I mean God's good desires, God's generous and loving desires for the earth. So if we say there is something deeply wrong with the way human beings are living, my primary concern is how we can begin to heal that and live in a better way for ourselves, for the earth, and for future generations. As for what happens when we die, if we're speaking of heaven, I feel like I understand less about that than I ever did before. But here's what I feel. I feel in my deepest bones that God is trustworthy. And I expect that when I reach my last breath I'll feel as I do now, that God is trustworthy. When I exhale my last exhalation, I trust that I will say, as Jesus did, 'Into your hands I commend my spirit, I commend who and what I am.' I trust God, and whatever happens is just fine with me. All those very material images we've been given of heaven – streets of gold, harps, thrones, all of that – that's just imagery. The imagery is there to evoke certain things in us. They're not necessarily giving us an accurate, objective understanding of what happens after life. But they're motivating us to live with hopeful resilience in this life. So we think of someone like Harriet Tubman or Dr King in the US, or Nelson Mandela and Desmond Tutu in South Africa, and so many others through history. These people knew they were risking their lives to try to help God's dream come true on earth as in heaven. They faced the dangers and said, look, I'm entrusting myself to God, and if I live a shorter life on this earth to do what's right, I'll gladly do that and trust myself to God afterwards. I don't feel I'll be wasting my life, I feel I'll be investing in a future of unending progression.

So many of our concepts of eternity, I'm now convinced, come to us from Greek philosophy. These concepts weren't native to the Jewish people at all. The Jewish people had virtually no interest or concern in the afterlife. Most still do not. All through the Hebrew Scriptures, there is no idea of going to heaven or hell after you die. (You may think so if you read the King James Version that includes a bad translation of the Hebrew word *sheol*.) So to me, death is a given, a fact of life. It's a natural and meaningful part of life. And it challenges me to take this breath, this moment, this day even more seriously. So rather than saying these years are a drop in the bucket, the fact that death is real means that when I woke up this morning, I had the chance to be with you today, for this precious time, to realize what a gift this is, what an irreplaceable day this is. As the psalm says, 'This is the day the LORD has made, let us rejoice and be glad in it.' In the last several years, I've walked both my parents up to the doorway of death and been their primary caretaker as they died. And when some of us, through illness or injury, or just old age, get to the point where we think, 'I've had enough of life, there's so much pain day after day after day', at that point, we're ready to say, 'I trust myself to God; I've had my turn here, and whatever's next I'm ready for it.' And we have confidence and peace rather than fear or denial.

In the United States we have our own uniquely ugly history of racism. Folk in the United Kingdom also have issues to deal with in this; they're quite different from ours. But our racial histories have common roots, and these roots go back very, very far. If you wanted a key day that relatively few Christians are aware of, it would not be 1492 but 1452. In the 1450s, Pope Nicholas V sent a letter, first to the king of Portugal and then to the king and queen of Spain, and then to the king of France, and to a number of other kings. These documents together are now known as the Doctrine of Discovery. The original one that was sent to the king of Portugal you can read in five minutes. It gives permission to all the Christian kings of Europe to go into all the world and make slaves of all nations and steal all their property and wealth. If they become Christians, then you'll have one relationship with them. If they do not become Christians, you have permission to do whatever you need to do to expropriate their wealth, including killing them and enslaving them. The whole history of colonialism flows from this – and here it is, all set out in the name of Christianity.

Since most of the Christians listening to the pope were white Europeans, Christian supremacy became the cover for white supremacy. This is an inescapable fact: that Western Christian history is interwoven with white supremacy. James Baldwin said, 'Not everything that is faced, can be overcome, but nothing can be changed until it is faced.' Now is our opportunity to face these things. I used to be afraid that the church would die, because it wasn't willing to change. Now I'm more worried that it will survive without changing the things that need to be changed, and that even more harm and damage could be done in the future – damage to the earth, damage to the poor, and damage in relation to race. I was part of the clergy witness in Charlottesville, Virginia, in 2017. I was there for the events of that day. We can talk about a pandemic virus. But we're having to face some of the spiritual viruses embedded in our culture, and passed on from generation to generation by breath; not by a physical virus but by sick words and attitudes that spread from mouth to ear and infect people's hearts with white Christian supremacy. This virus goes on generation after generation, and its death toll is shockingly high and could go far higher, which is why I wrote my newest book, *Do I Stay Christian?*

This is such a deep-seated problem. And we've only just described the Christian version of it in the West. But if we were in India, the caste system has certain similarities. If we were in Rwanda and Burundi, the relationship between Tutsi and Hutu has similar patterns, and Christianity had an influence on some of those dynamics for the worse. So around the world this is a human problem: some people like to gain power over others, and they like to get their own gains, even at the expense of others.

And this is where the basic teaching of Jesus is challenging us. Jesus says to love your neighbour, not beneath yourself but as yourself. So everything you want for yourself, you want for your neighbour. This deeply Christian paradigm shift is what we need.

Imagine if I were to go to my Jewish friends and say to them, 'What do you wish we Christians would do about the long Christian history of anti-Semitism?' In other words, instead of starting with our own think-ing, I'd like to start with the thinking of the people who are experiencing the harm done by some of our Christian practices and attitudes. Simi-larly, imagine going to our Muslim neighbours and saying, 'Knowing what you've seen of our relationship over many centuries, what do you Muslims wish we would do to improve our relationship?'

I think we have to do something very similar in the issue of race. If we're white, instead of thinking, 'What do we white people think we should do?', we should listen humbly to what our Black and brown and Asian and indigenous brothers and sisters want to say to us. The act of listening is one of the changes that's needed so much, you see – instead of white people running off thinking we can solve it without building a relationship of humble listening to the people our religion has harmed. We have to try to build those relationships. That means for all of us, especially those in a position of privilege, that we have to go prepared not to be respected, not to be trusted. We have to be prepared to have people be suspicious of us because they have a longstanding reason to be. Listening and entering into relationship, even though we're starting not at zero but at minus ten: there's no shortcut around that. We have to start in the mess we inherited.

I say this jokingly, but I mean it seriously: I feel we should give all of our religious leaders a promotion. Our archbishops and popes and presiding bishops should all become interfaith ambassadors: their main job is to build relationships with other faiths, and then let everybody else move up and fill in the gaps. Because we need our leaders to be leading in the work of conciliation and reconciliation, of peacemaking through the facing of our past, so we can work together to build a better future. Every one of us has a role to play in that blessed work of being peacemakers.

You think of St Francis having the courage to go into the Sultan of Egypt's camp during the Crusades, not to proclaim supremacy and to threaten his life but to go and say: 'Hey, we have to meet one another in peace. My following of Jesus requires me to live in peace. Your following of the Qur'an requires the same of you. How can we live in peace?'

To approach one another in this Franciscan spirit, we'll need to purge some unhealthy elements from our theology. Lesslie Newbigin, the great British missiologist, said that the greatest heresy in the history of monotheism is the misunderstanding of election, the idea of being chosen by God. We have taught that election is for privilege – when election is for service. You're not chosen to get benefits and prizes and cake, you're chosen to go and be a servant of all. That's an easy sentence to say. But if we were to take Newbigin's brilliant and radical insight, and really let it work on us, I think it would take us just where we need to go.

Nobody else is going to fix all this for us. If we're waiting for a new Martin Luther, or Paul, or even Jesus, to come and fix everything, we will become part of the problem. We all must be Martin Luther. Rather than waiting for a new Paul to arise, we need to follow Paul's example. Of course, this is what Jesus said. 'You are my body,' he said. 'I will live in you.' So we have to fix it together – empowered by the indwelling Spirit. We have to echo Moses when he said, 'I wish all the Lord's people were prophets.' All of us are going to have to step into that role in our own way, and stop waiting for a superhero to fly in and fix everything with a magic wand or superpower. If there is a superpower, it's very simple, very down to earth: it's love – love expressed in each of us, in the way we live and work and serve, day after day.

This is what Jesus did. He was just one person, using his one voice, speaking the message that God put in his heart. First a few, then hundreds, then thousands and thousands of people would gather on a hillside to get a chance to listen to him. And St Francis was just one person. First a few, then hundreds, then thousands of people started hearing about him and feeling inspired to follow his way of life. A generation before St Francis, there was Hildegard von Bingen. She was just one woman, in a time when women weren't given much respect. But she just went ahead and did what was in her heart, including all kinds of things that women weren't allowed to do. And word spread. Her influence, her spirit, her creativity and courage inspired others. So it doesn't take much. A little light from one person can shine brightly and inspire others. It's already happening. But it could happen much more. People's scepticism about good things coming from the Christian faith is warranted. They have reasons to be sceptical; which means we ought to expect we have to do the right thing for a long time before we should expect people to notice, because we've got an awful lot of negative history. We're not starting at zero. We're starting at minus ten or minus fifty.

Imagine a young parent who has young children. One of them has just made a mess, another one is throwing up on the floor, a third is screaming and crying because his brother took his toy. It just seems like total chaos. At that moment the parent can think, 'I must be a terrible parent, because my children are crying, and they're unhappy, and they're grumpy.' But what we want to say is, 'No, this is just part of life. These are wonderful children, and better days will come. All shall be well. You'll get through this rough night. The costs of parenthood are great, but the joys of parenthood are great as well. And this is life. The love you have for your children at this moment is part of the beauty of this moment: the fact that, at their worst, you still love them.' God is real in the mess and difficulty of life. These are opportunities for love and forgiveness to flow and resilience and creativity to flow. Those are all good things. Julian's 'All shall be well' might not mean 'All shall be easy', but it will mean what it meant that first creation day. What is may be chaotic and unfinished. But there is good today. And tomorrow, there will be more good. And eventually, it will be very good, very good indeed.

14 October 2021

Epilogue

What has the Spirit been saying to the churches during the pandemic? When there's an urgent crisis, a new hierarchy develops to suit the new circumstances. Top of the tree are those too frantically busy saving or rescuing to stop and explain. Not far away are those who have diagnosed, deconstructed and pronounced, regardless of whether the key facts are known. Bottom of the hierarchy are those who are caught up in it but don't know what to do or how to be helpful.

In March 2020 the churches discovered some home truths. They wanted to be in category one, frantically busy, with the key workers. As it happened, clergy woke up at the start of the pandemic and discovered we weren't key workers. We could shout and scream how important we were, but no one was really listening. Some churches and theologians were happy to be in category two, pronouncing wisdom, undaunted by our lack of knowledge of what this pandemic was, how serious it would get or how long it would last. Most of that wisdom, as in many crises, was empty. What churches found hardest was being in category three – not knowing what to do or how to be helpful. What have we learned in the last two years? I'm going to suggest five lessons.

Number one: no one likes a moaner – still less, a self-important moaner. There's no point telling the world how important you are and insisting that, for you, nothing must change, even though the whole world is having to make endless adaptations. Very little about what we're attached to about church is basic to what church is. The New Testament says little about buildings, not much about service times or styles of music, and nothing about the liturgical year. But it says a great deal about eating together, washing one another's feet, every member having a role to play, making sacrifices, and God providing for the community as it faces each new challenge. Necessity is the mother of invention, and those who've found a way through the last two years have been those who've improvised, adapted and enjoyed the challenge of making old things work in new circumstances.

Number two: the secret of happiness is to enjoy what God is giving in abundance, not to pine for what is scarce. If the church is closed, this is a moment for discovering the remarkable things like online compline or guided prayer walks or live-streamed choral music. If you can't be one body together because of covid regulations, find another way to be one body. Discover new skills from community members who were well down the pre-pandemic pecking order, but can now teach the tech-averse to surf, or the medically challenged to lateral flow. Rejoice at the people who find you online whom you'd never find in person.

Number three: generosity is best investment. People were drawn to the early church because Christians loved one another, not because they claimed they were immune to a virus or demanded their building be an exception or saw every government regulation as part of a sinister expansion of state surveillance. The best evangelism is what it has always been – selfless acts of kindness and thoughtfulness that suggest something wonderful is happening in your heart that I'd rather like to be happening in mine. Be humbled by those who gave up their personal time to supervise vaccine queues. Be inspired by those who delivered food, or rang isolated neighbours, or ran Zoom bereavement groups, or offered weekly connection and food hubs for asylum seekers. Call me old-fashioned, but that's what Christians do. We're not an interest group, defending our rights. We're defined by washing feet. After all, 'Love your neighbour as yourself' is supposed to mean 'Look out for those whom the pandemic has hit hardest, and make their needs at least as central as your own convenience in calculating priorities and responses.'

Number four: times of hardship renew God's people. It's when things are difficult that we rediscover who God is and who we are. We find surprising partners and friends. We find the gifts God brings us through the stranger. We find new joy in faith when it feels like it really matters, not just for ever but right now. We realize our tiny choices of whether to wear a mask, or take a lateral flow, or have an in-person meeting have public significance – we're not atomized individuals, we're part of a social body, and its workings are determined not by government but by the solidarity of common understanding and the shared shouldering of irritating disciplines. We don't seek out a safe treehouse where we're immune and above and beyond: we face the realities of death, disruption and depression together. We get so deeply interdependent with one another that in 20 years' time we bore our grandchildren with the spirit of the pandemic the way our grandparents bored us about not locking their doors during the war.

Number five: God is still God. If we can't share the wine at the Eucharist, the Holy Spirit finds another way to be in communion with us. If we can't sing in church, the Holy Spirit finds another way to sing God's song of joy and reversal to us. If God doesn't seem so churchy when we're all isolating, then maybe it's time to re-encounter the God made known in the lilies of the field and the birds of the air. Never shrink the boundless scope and relentless longing of God to the mundane habits and limited imagination of church. Just remember the main points of the news, according to Paul – love, joy, peace, patience, kindness, goodness, faithfulness, gentleness and self-control. Have any of those been abolished by the pandemic, been rendered impossible, or become irrelevant? Or have we actually had more opportunities to exercise them and grow in them than ever before?

I may be dreaming, but this is what I would like the rest of society to be saying about church once the pandemic is over. 'Isn't it great that there are people who selflessly give up their time to sit in the building or on Zoom with those who are isolated, who freely offer to support young people whose schooling has been disrupted, who are glad to walk with those who experience mental illness without judgement or hasty solutions but with patience and love? Isn't it amazing that there are people whose faith is so great that their attitude to public health isn't dominated by their own convenience or circumstances, but who see the pandemic as a chance to rediscover our common purpose as one people? Isn't it impressive that there are people who aren't overshadowed by what they can't do, but who embody and inspire others to discover what they *can* do that they never tried doing before? Isn't it remarkable that, surrounded as we are by lament and grief and resentment and loss, there are people who truly believe in a future that's bigger than the past – a future God is bringing often despite our faltering efforts? Isn't it wonderful that people do these things not to impress anybody but simply content that God sees, and smiles, because these are God's ways?'

The pandemic isn't over yet. That's a bad thing for our sense of progress and purpose. But it's a good thing if we realize there's still time to rescue how the pandemic is remembered. Will it be recalled as the time the churches shrank into their own narrow needs and personal predilections and faltering fears? I truly hope not. There's still time for it to be remembered as the season people of faith rediscovered who they fundamentally are, and how they could demonstrate that identity in a way that inspired all around them. It's not too late – if we really want to.

11 *January* 2022

References and Further Reading

Alexander, Michelle, 2012, *The New Jim Crow: Mass Incarceration in the Age of Colourblindness*, The New Press.

Cone, James, 2013, *The Cross and the Lynching Tree*, Orbis Books.

Hauerwas, Stanley, 1981, *A Community of Character: Towards a Constructive Christian Social Ethic*, University of Notre Dame Press.

Hauerwas, Stanley, 1995, *Dispatches from the Front: Theological Engagements with the Secular*, Duke University Press.

Hauerwas, Stanley, 1977, *Truthfulness and Tragedy: Further Investigations in Christian Ethics*, University of Notre Dame Press.

Hauerwas, Stanley, 1981, *Vision and Virtue: Essays in Christian Ethical Reflection*, University of Notre Dame Press.

Hauerwas, Stanley, 2015, *The Work of Theology*, Wm. B. Eerdmans.

Hauerwas, Stanley and Samuel Wells, 2006, *Blackwell Companion to Christian Ethics*, Blackwell Publishing.

James, William, 1982, *The Varieties of Religious Experience: A Study in Human Nature*, Penguin Classics.

Lindsay, Ben, 2019, *We Need to Talk about Race: Understanding the Black Experience in White Majority Churches*, SPCK.

MacIntyre, Alastair, 2007, *After Virtue: A Study in Moral Theory*, University of Notre Dame Press.

Marquand, David, 2015, *Mammon's Kingdom: An Essay on Britain*, Penguin.

McDonald, Chine, 2021, *God is Not a White Man: And Other Revelations*, Hodder & Stoughton.

McLaren, Brian, 2022, *Do I Stay Christian?: A Guide for the Doubters, the Disappointed and the Disillusioned*, Hodder & Stoughton.

McLaren, Brian, 2021, *Faith after Doubt: Why Your Beliefs Stopped Working and What to Do About It*, Hodder & Stoughton.

Niebuhr, H. Richard, 2002, *Christ and Culture*, Harper Collins.

Orwell, George, 2000, *Animal Farm*, Penguin Classics.

Suhard, Emmanuel, 2011, *Priests Among Men*, Literary Licensing, LLC.

Temple, William, 1976, *Christianity and the Social Order*, Shepheard-Walwyn Publisher.

Thurman, Howard, 1996, *Jesus and the Disinherited*, Beacon Press.

Tran, Jonathan, 2022, *Asian Americans and the Spirit of Racial Capitalism*, Oxford University Press.

von Balthasar, Hans Urs, 1982, *Seeing the Form: A Theological Aesthetics*, Ignatius Press.

Wells, Samuel, 2004, *Improvisation: The Drama of Christian Ethics*, SPCK.

Wells, Samuel and Stanley Hauerwas, *In Conversation: Samuel Wells and Stanley Hauerwas*, Church Publishing.

Wilbur, Richard, 1989, 'For Dudley', in *New and Collected Poems*, Harcourt Brace Jovanovich.

CPSIA information can be obtained
at www.ICGtesting.com
Printed in the USA
BVHW030118310123
657442BV00006B/379